EXPLOITS
OF A REAL
ATF AGENT

Exploits of a Real ATF Agent

By
Cal Campbell

E-BookTime, LLC
Montgomery, Alabama

Exploits of a Real ATF Agent

Library of Congress Control Number: 2012949521

ISBN: 978-1-60862-431-7

First Edition
Published September 2012
E-BookTime, LLC
6598 Pumpkin Road
Montgomery, AL 36108
www.e-booktime.com

Dedication

The author would like to dedicate this book to the brave men and women who are presently serving as agents for the ATF.

The agents are an elite group of individuals often sacrificing their normal family life to serve the citizens of this great country.

With the threat of terrorists, the roles of the present day agents are far more dangerous and sophisticated than when my father served as an ATF agent.

The exception, perhaps, is when Charlie Campbell first served as a Prohibition agent.

Preface 9

Prologue *The Prohibition Era* 11

Chapter 1 *Elk Point, South Dakota* 15
Chapter 2 *Charlie Becomes an Agent* 21
Chapter 3 *Undercover Agent: West Virginia* 27
Chapter 4 *Rum Runners: Key West* 33
Chapter 5 *Return to Chicago* 47
Chapter 6 *Witness Protection* 55
Chapter 7 *The Trial of Little John* 63
Chapter 8 *The Peaceful Years* 65
Chapter 9 *The Canadian Connection* 69
Chapter 10 *The North Star Raid* 77
Chapter 11 *The Sand Hills of Nebraska* 83
Chapter 12 *Illegal Hooch: Close to Home* 89
Chapter 13 *Trouble at the Pine Ridge Indian
                 Reservation* 97
Chapter 14 *Charlie's Visit to His Brother* 101
Chapter 15 *Trouble in Eastern South Dakota* 105
Chapter 16 *The Terrorist in Kansas* 111
Chapter 17 *Conclusion* 121

Epilogue *Modern Expectations of an ATF Agent* 127

Photographs 131

Letters of Commendation, Promotion, and Awards
for Charles E. Campbell, Federal Agent, Alcohol,
Tobacco and Firearms, Treasury Department 155

Prologue

The Prohibition Era

In the beginning of the 20th century, there were Temperance organizations in nearly every state. By 1916, over half of the states already had statutes that prohibited buying and selling alcohol.

Due to increased pressure, President Herbert Hoover outlawed alcohol, and the American Mob was born. In the opinion of many, the Mob was given the greatest cash cow in history – illegal liquor.

Few people stopped drinking. But rival gangs began fighting for territory, since members of each gang wanted to control as many blocks in the large cities as possible. As a result, innocents were caught between merciless rival Irish, Jewish, and Italian gangs.

It was only a few years later, when the lawmakers in Washington realized that they were giving away millions of dollars in taxes, that they repealed the Volstead Act. As you probably know, in 1919 the 18th

Amendment to the U.S. Constitution, which prohibited the sale and manufacture of alcohol, was ratified. It went into effect on January 16, 1920.

The lax law enforcement in New York allowed the Sicilian gangs, along with the Jewish and Irish bootleggers, to abandon their primitive cookers and develop more sophisticated and more profitable techniques in producing their illegal booze. In addition to brewing their own product, these entrepreneurs were able to smuggle quality liquor from Canada and Great Britain, while opening their own covert businesses in the United States.

Profits from the illegal breweries were huge. While each barrel of beer cost somewhat less than five dollars to produce, the barrel netted about $36 upon delivery to a speakeasy.

Fortunately, or perhaps not, the gangs often fought over territory. Many lives were lost and families were torn apart as greed took over in many major U.S. cities. However, Al Capone, Chicago's Italian Mob boss, and the other Mafia Dons decided on a truce and divided the city of Chicago so that each Mafia family realized a profit from its illegal activities.

Before the end of 1931, the New York bosses traveled to Chicago for a national conference with Capone. The leaders of more than twenty other Mafia units all attended the meeting. The reason for the meeting was so "Lucky" Luciano could explain his concept for avoiding intra-family and inter-family mob wars. It was Luciano's idea that each family on the Mafia

Commission would have a single vote. Therefore, all decisions determined by the majority would be final with no debate. The Commission voted on the rules that would be followed. If the set of rules was not followed, the other families would settle the score. The Mafia Commission voted on who would control which territories and what illegal activities the Mob would be allowed to indulge in with the Commission's protection.

Chicago's secret meeting ended at the Blackstone Hotel. On the last evening, Al Capone hosted a feast where delegates participated in wine and women. He had arranged for a number of prostitutes to attend the gala event. The feds had no hint of the meeting, but the long-term effects would vastly strengthen the Mafia. The results of this high-level meeting had very significant outcomes, as there were now guidelines established so that each family would make a profit without interference from the other Mob families.

Chapter 1

Elk Point, South Dakota

Charlie Campbell's attempt at farming fell short of the family's expectations, as crop after crop failed in the barren prairie of northwest South Dakota.

Charlie's parents had traveled by covered wagon to South Dakota from southern Iowa, all the time hoping to make life better for their six children. As the one hundred sixty acres given to "homesteaders" by the United States Government in 1862 was not enough land to support the large family, Charlie and his new wife, Beulah, thought about other careers to pursue.

Since Charlie was a big man who had a reputation of being very good with his fists and defeating all aspiring boxers in the area, he thought that he could easily apply and obtain the job as the only police officer in the small town of Elk Point, South Dakota. Perhaps the reason that the city council and mayor agreed to hire Charlie was that in addition to obtaining a very big and apparently strong man, Charlie brought his German Shepherd dog with him to patrol this tiny town in southeastern South Dakota.

Well, Charlie had no trouble with the small town's roughnecks and drunks; not because of his reputation, but because of Gary, the largest German Shepherd dog that they had witnessed in that part of the state. Together, they would patrol the city, and each evening, walk the streets to see that the store owners had locked their establishments. Occasionally, it would be necessary to arrest a drunk and disorderly citizen and let the fellow spend the night in the local two-cell jail.

Charlie was always conscious of his health and prided himself on his fine physique. In fact, he would wrap metal chains around a broomstick, and each morning, as a workout, lift the heavy object at least twenty times. He would also jog short distances on the country roads to improve his endurance. Being six feet tall with broad shoulders, bulging biceps, and a rugged look about him, nobody wanted to "mess" with the new policeman who took over the town of Elk Point. Although he wore glasses, he could see just fine without them.

The only shortcoming that Charlie had was his temper, and on more than one occasion, he would use the butt of his .38 special to pistol-whip a disorderly individual who refused to follow directions.

As the job of city policeman was somewhat boring to Charlie, he would occasionally drive to Sioux City, Iowa, to attend the prize fights that were held on weekends. On one trip to Sioux City, he was at a local drinking establishment and met a group of men obtaining autographs from a big man sitting at a table in the corner. Always a curious sort of guy, Charlie ambled over to the table and introduced himself to Jack Dempsey. He was told that the weekend fight scheduled for Saturday night might need to be cancelled as Mr. Dempsey's opponent had not arrived on the afternoon train.

It should be known that the year was 1918, one year prior to Jack Dempsey winning the world heavyweight title. Charlie, now thirty-one years old, always in the need for money, asked how much would be paid if he fought Mr. Dempsey for one round. Mr. Dempsey's manager looked over Charlie's muscular six-foot frame and thought, *"Well, why not give this 'hayseed' a chance to get busted up by my fighter? Anyway, we can make a few bucks from the fight."*

As Charlie already had a reputation of being a good amateur fighter in this area of South Dakota and Iowa, there were side bets that maybe, just maybe, Charlie could prove himself in the ring with this famous fighter.

Charlie had to borrow fighting shorts and gloves from the Dempsey entourage. One of the men with the Dempsey party asked if Charlie was a "bleeder." Charlie thought to himself that although he had been hit in the head a few times, his constant weaving and dodging prevented any opponents from landing a solid punch to the face. Therefore, he did not know if he was prone to bleeding when hit in the face.

As Jack Dempsey had quite a reputation as a fighter, the high school gym where the fight was to be held was packed with both locals from Sioux City and the surrounding area. As the fight progressed and Charlie was holding his own, and also landing a few solid punches to both Dempsey's body and face, the manager thought about calling the fight before disaster overtook this famous fighter. Neither fighter had been knocked to the mat, but it was obvious that Charlie was soon dominating the fight.

After one round, the manager called the fight a draw and pulled Jack from the ring. Perhaps one reason for only one round was that Charlie had connected with a left upper-cut that bloodied Jack's upper lip. As a result, there was a constant round of "boos" from the assembled throng. The locals thought that Charlie should have at least been allowed to fight a bit longer.

Since only one round had been fought and the decision was a draw, little money changed hands. However, Dempsey and his group, with police escort, quickly made their way out of town to catch the last train leaving Sioux City that night.

Upon returning home, Beulah noticed that her handsome husband had a swollen eye and a cut lip. Beulah didn't say anything, as she thought that perhaps he had gotten into a bar fight.

Charlie never told his new bride what had happened that night. Instead, he pocketed the ten dollars given to him by Dempsey's manager. After all, ten dollars could

18

buy his favorite whiskey and a few packs of Lucky Strikes – his favorite cigarette.

It was seldom that Beulah ever questioned what her husband, Charlie, was doing, as she knew that many of his operations needed to be kept confidential. This was the case when Charlie returned from Sioux City.

The only trouble that Charlie had to deal with as a police officer in Elk Point was one night when a snatch-and-grab thief broke the front window of the only jewelry store in town and made off with the watches, rings, and bracelets. Charlie had told the store owner, Angus Larson, that he should empty the front showcase every night. However, being a stubborn Swede, Angus would seldom listen to anyone who offered suggestions.

Charlie's pay was minimal, and his duties were getting to be so routine that he started to think about other jobs in law enforcement.

Chapter 2

Charlie Becomes an Agent

Charlie decided to apply for a job as a federal agent to enforce Prohibition. This kind of career should pay more and be more exciting.

With the encouragement of Beulah, his young wife, he took a train to Chicago to apply for the position.

As the federal agency in charge of enforcing this new law had to recruit many agents in a short period of time, the credentials of many applicants were overlooked. The result was the hiring of many under-qualified and under-paid agents. Therefore, it was not surprising that there was a high rate of bribery in order to obtain jobs.

However, Charlie Campbell had always had high moral standards and would not accept money for "looking the other way." In fact, later he received praise from Eliot Ness.

Now, Charlie had not graduated from high school, as he had to work on his parents' farm. But with his law enforcement background as the constable of Elk Point, South Dakota, he received the position of agent under the direction of the Treasury Department in 1925.

Beulah was proud of her husband's new job and decided that since his new responsibilities would require unlimited traveling, she should stay in Elk Point where she had friends, and her parents were nearby.

Charlie's first duty did not take him far from home. He was assigned to Yankton, South Dakota, to perform as an undercover agent in the hopes of locating some bootleggers. Charlie was told to buy the "evidence" and store it – in this case, in the mayor's basement.

Aided by local, state, and county lawmen, who were always cooperative, they raided taverns and homes where evidence had been established. Charlie learned later that bootleggers would as soon shoot a man as look at him. After learning the dangers of the job, he not only carried his .38 pistol, which he carried in a side holster, he also obtained a small pistol that he strapped to his thick right ankle.

The leading kingpin of this criminal element led back to Al Capone. It was also during this time that the Mafia was strengthened, as there was money to be made from prostitution, gambling, and illegal alcohol sales.

Charlie's second assignment was in up-state New York. There, he was to watch for trucks moving illegal liquor from Canada. A group of agents would travel to the state line and wait in the dark of night to watch for the movement of a convoy of vehicles crossing into the United States.

Ironic as it may seem, sometimes rival gangs would hijack the trucks before they reached the location of the waiting federal agents. Charlie thought to himself that perhaps someone in the agency had tipped off the rival gang so that they could move closer to the Canadian border and confiscate the booze.

During the rare times that they were able to seize a convoy of trucks carrying the booze, the agents would unload the barrels of liquor, and with axes, break apart the load and let the liquid soak into the ground. What a waste! It took nearly two years to control this illegal activity.

Charlie earned a brief vacation before his next assignment in Chicago. There, he performed the work of others, with Eliot Ness as their boss.

One assignment Charlie had was to raid the speakeasies and arrest the management and patrons, and in the process, destroy the liquor found. Sometimes, after entering these establishments, the agents would find the customers watching the strippers and drinking soft drinks. There was no alcohol in sight. Obviously, someone in the agency had tipped off the speakeasy about a planned raid, and a thorough cleanup had been done.

After eighteen months, Charlie became so disgusted with the corruption in Chicago that he asked for a transfer to another city. The district office complied with his request and transferred Charlie to Omaha,

Nebraska, where he continued to enforce Prohibition laws. This move was to Charlie's delight as he could be closer to his wife, Beulah, and by then, their two small children, who were still living in Elk Point, South Dakota.

Charlie's supervisor in Omaha thought that since he had requested a transfer from Chicago, that perhaps he was a troublemaker. Therefore, Bernie, the supervisor in this district, gave Charlie all of the rotten jobs.

One morning as Charlie was reporting to the office, Bernie said that he had heard that Charlie thought there might have been members of their elite group who had leaked information to the gangs of Chicago. Therefore, he had just the job for Charlie – to assign him to listen to a wiretap that was installed in a hangout of the criminals, right there in Omaha. The purpose of the wiretap was to record incriminating information about the location of the illegal liquor.

The listening post was in a roach-infested, rundown hotel across the street from the gang's favorite Italian restaurant. Boy, when Bernie gets your number, you are in for a lot of crap!

Not only did Charlie and his partner have to take shifts staying awake and eating "take out" food from a not-so-great Chinese restaurant that a third agent brought to them, the two agents could not see their families for at least a couple of weeks. Of course, writing letters was also forbidden. Charlie thought that being an agent might not have been the best career move.

It was getting to the point that neither agent could take any more Chinese food. For the rest of his life, Charlie could not even walk past an oriental restaurant without getting sick to his stomach.

Charlie's supervisor, Bernie, did not know that Charlie's mother's last name was Ferraro. During Charlie's early years, he sat on his mother's knee and learned to speak Italian. Therefore, during the weeks on the wiretap, Charlie was able to pick up a lot of information that other agents were not able to understand.

The wiretap was a success, and the agents, with the compliance of the state's attorney, raided the warehouse where most of the illegal liquor was being stored. They also were able to obtain the names of a few key gangsters in several cities who were later arrested. Now, Bernie had thought the agents he had put on the wiretap would not be successful in obtaining any information. The rumor that Bernie thought that nothing would come of this stakeout made Charlie suspect that Bernie was indeed the "rotten apple" leaking information to the Mob.

The loss of a large quantity of the liquor put a sizeable dent in the distribution of the spirits to Omaha's speakeasies and elsewhere. However, it didn't take long for the supply to be reestablished, and the gangs were once again in operation. The agents, of course, thought that the time spent listening on the wiretap was a waste of time.

Again, Charlie applied for a transfer so that he could get out of the reaches of Bernie. Now, a hostile relationship had developed between the two men. It was still in the back of Charlie's mind that Bernie was the source of the leaks to the criminal element. However, nothing was proven, and so Charlie moved on with his career. But the idea of a snitch in the Bureau stayed with Charlie, and later, proof did come in an unexpected way.

Chapter 3

Undercover Agent: West Virginia

It seemed that the assignments that Charlie was given had become more undesirable all the time. Now, a couple of Charlie's supervisors from Washington, D.C. visited Omaha and announced, not asked, that Charlie's new assignment would be as an undercover agent in the rural settlement of Petersburg, West Virginia. There had been reports of the mountains containing numerous stills.

Charlie was to arrive in Petersburg as a known criminal. He was assigned an old beat-up jalopy to drive.

Of course, the agency had an elaborate plan. The Bureau knew that Charlie could not develop the broken West Virginia accent in a short period of time. Therefore, the Bureau established a criminal record for Charlie with a false name and credentials. This included false papers and his "mug" on a wanted poster that would be placed in the local post office.

Charlie asked who his contact would be and what job he would have in Petersburg. The agent in charge of "handling" Charlie told him not to worry about the contact. He would be informed of the plan at a later date.

In the meantime, they knew that Charlie had developed a skill as an auto mechanic. Really, all farmers needed to be able to fix their machines, and Charlie had been a farmer before he became a law enforcement agent. Therefore, Charlie was to apply at the only garage in this small town and show them his skills as a mechanic. There was little doubt that Charlie could fix anything that was brought into this small garage, so he was hired.

For the first day of his new job, Charlie appeared with grease-covered overalls. In his bib pocket, he carried his usual plug of Horseshoe chewing tobacco. He purposely had not shaved for a week and had let the chewing tobacco stick between his teeth this first morning on the job. Also, Charlie thought to himself, *"Why should I comb my hair today? The hell with it."*

Many of the agents had started chewing tobacco since the light from a cigarette would give away their location when they hid in the brush waiting for the convoys of trucks along the Canadian border.

One of the supervising agents told Charlie that his new name was now Lester. It was then that Charlie remarked that he knew good ole boys down there used their first and middle name. He asked about using the name of Billie Bob. The supervising agent laughed and reminded Charlie that he was from Illinois and running from authorities. Therefore, he would have only one name.

Charlie asked about his last name. The Bureau had already given Lester the last name of Smith. Charlie thought to himself, *"Now that is really original; just like the Bureau to be dumb asses and come up with such a common name."*

Charlie was soon able to gain the trust of the local "good ole boys" by drinking moonshine with them in the evening at the only bar in this small, rural town. In order to keep up with the locals in downing the rot-gut booze, he would have a greasy, heavy meal before beginning his drinking with the locals. In this way, he could appear a little tipsy, but still keep his wits about him. He soon learned to like opossum gravy.

During the day, he worked at the local garage doing his best to repair cars of those few residents in this small, God-forsaken town that only anyone born in these parts would appreciate. One day, an obvious boot-legger's 1920 Chevy Touring car came in for repairs. After admiring the car, Lester told the local that he was sure that a car like that would be easy to repair as he had used a car similar to this one in holding up banks in Illinois.

The driver, after looking over Lester, asked him if he would like a job delivering a few cases of moonshine to a home in Medley. He had already checked out Lester from his buddies whom he drank with at the local bar. Charlie thought to himself that he had better deliver this first run of moonshine before informing his contact for a bust. By doing this, he would establish some trust so that he could find the location of the still.

It was a good thing that Charlie had not informed his contact, as this was a test, and there really was not any moonshine in the concealed tanks of the car. Rather, the cunning bastards had placed water in the tanks that had been installed in the trunk, behind the back seat, and in back of the dash board.

After this first successful run, the group of moonshiners began to trust Lester and gave him a second run to Medley with the moonshine. It was at this point that Charlie contacted the Bureau by using the telephone booth outside a local bar. As anyone could be listening on this line, the agents talked in a code they had developed earlier.

Charlie was able to convince his contacts that if he were sighted by the feds making this delivery, they should let him outrun them. This successful delivery would further gain the trust of the gang.

It was a full month later that Charlie was instructed to drive to the location of the still in the remote mountains to pick up yet a third round of alcohol and deliver it to Medley. Now it was time to call the feds and give them the location of the still.

After Charlie had picked up the liquor and was making the run to Medley, the agents raided the still. By being away from the site of the still, Charlie did not blow his cover.

After discovering three more remote stills in the mountains and having them raided, he and his contact thought it was time for Lester to disappear, as it was too much of a coincidence that three stills were discovered after Lester arrived.

The good ole boys had become somewhat suspicious of Charlie, and it was a good thing that Charlie had decided to get out of town in the middle of the night. Luck would have it that on the night he left, there was no moon. However, as Charlie was slowly pulling out of town, the damn coon hounds let out a howl that everyone in town heard. As the gang had already become suspicious, they knew that the hounds were not just howling at a raccoon.

As Charlie was about a mile out of town, he heard a shotgun blast and was aware of the pellets hitting his side of the car. Now the race was on to see who would be the best driver on the mountain curves. Charlie thought to himself, *"Those sons-a-bitches will get me yet."*

It was well into the morning when Charlie reached the main blacktop and considered himself out of the reaches of the red-neck mountain men.

Charlie now earned a month's vacation and returned to Elk Point for time with his family.

About a month later, Charlie was ordered to the capital, Charleston, West Virginia, to testify against the moonshiners. Boy, when Charlie appeared in court with his three-piece suit and shined shoes, there was a hush by the spectators. The local police allowed this federal agent to keep his .38 pistol strapped to his chest as there had been a hit ordered on him.

The locals knew better than to tangle with Charlie, as they had witnessed him knocking down a couple of their best after a bar fight. In addition to seeing the outline of the pistol strapped just under his suit jacket, he was also accompanied by two other federal agents and one state trooper.

After the trial that resulted in guilty verdicts, Charlie was escorted out the back door of the court-house, and striding along beside him was his security detail. Again, Charlie thought to himself, *"Those hillbillies sure are a bunch of ignorant assholes. I hope to never again be assigned to the South."*

Chapter 4

Rum Runners: Key West

Charlie's new assignment was going to be Key West, Florida. This time he was to apprehend and arrest the rum runners who were shipping rum from Cuba into the U.S. Again, he thought to himself, *"That bastard Bernie is behind me getting assigned to all the rotten locations. I will continue to rely on my contacts and someday get the goods on him."*

After taking a bus to New York, and then on to St. Augustine, Florida, Charlie boarded Mr. Henry Flagler's train for the trip to Key West.

First, as passengers on Mr. Flagler's train were primarily wealthy vacationers from the East Coast, Charlie had to dress the part. It was necessary that he requisition appropriate up-scale resort wear so that he would not stand out from the other well-healed passengers.

It took a lot of arm twisting to obtain the necessary funds from the government to buy a single white suit and accessories. Charlie's supervisors finally agreed to release the money for their agent to buy the clothes. However, a telegram arrived about the time Charlie settled in Key West. The government insisted that Charlie have the suit cleaned and then mailed back to Washington. They also wanted the very stylish hat.

Riding on this fancy train that traveled on a bridge directly over the water, Charlie was fascinated at the sight, but he was also somewhat apprehensive. His knuckles were white as he grasped the seat arms, hoping that the train stayed on the track.

After getting off the train and with wobbly knees, Charlie first found a clothing store to change out of his white three-piece suit and bought a loud Key West shirt and appropriate pants. Of course, the next step was to find a cleaners and then a post office where he could send the expensive suit back to Washington.

With his new attire, Charlie did "blend in" with the natives on this isolated island.

Charlie was to meet his contact in a local hotel, the very up-scale Crowne Plaza La Concha. The contact was in room 301. After the coded three knocks, a pause, and then two more knocks, a Cuban by the name of Garcia slowly opened the door with the chain still attached.

Garcia seemed very nervous as he was serving as a well-paid informant. The agency did not have any Hispanic agents, and therefore, had to rely on bums like

Garcia to obtain information on the boats running liquor from Cuba to one of the islands just off the coast of Key West.

The plan quickly formed. Garcia was to inform Charlie and one other agent of the next "run" expected that next week. In the meantime, Charlie had to blend in with the locals. He still had not met his partner nor found a place to stay. However, he knew that he had to find a cheap hotel or rooming house, as staying at the Crowne Plaza La Concha would be too obvious for a stranger just arriving from the mainland. Furthermore, the department certainly would not pay for an agent staying in such an up-scale hotel.

Strolling down Duvall Street, Charlie noticed that a number of natives were either drinking or had obtained a new drug called marijuana, and were openly smoking the weed. He had been told by his superiors that they were to concentrate on the illegal alcohol and that maybe someday they would crack down on these other drugs.

Standing on the street corner, Charlie was approached by a young man no older than nineteen. Martino gave the agreed-upon password and introduced himself as his fellow agent. Charlie thought to himself, *"They must be desperate for agents to let a kid this young join the force."* However, the "kid" knew a lot about the islands surrounding the Keys, as he was born a Conch. Marino explained that a Conch was a native born in Key West.

Charlie asked what they should do to pass the time until Garcia informed them of when the next shipment of rum was being sent from Cuba. Martino suggested that they amble over to the auditorium and watch the fights. When they entered, neither agent recognized the referee in the ring.

Later, someone identified him as Ernest Hemingway. Ernest loved to watch boxing, and through persuasion, the locals had convinced him to act as the referee on this particular day.

The fights were somewhat brutal, and that seemed to excite the fans who loved the blood that each boxer extracted from the other. In fact, sitting in the second row, blood from one fighter splattered over the top of the ring and hit Charlie in the face.

Martino and Charlie learned sometime later, that in another part of town, they could have watched and bet on cock fights. Although these fights were illegal, it seemed that the local police could be bought for a price.

Both agents agreed that when Garcia gave them the information on the next "rum run," they could not rely on the local police for assistance. Charlie thought that with tommy guns and their .38 specials, they could make the arrests.

As the agents were leaving the boxing match, a beautiful Cuban girl passed by and said, *"Buenas tardes Martino,"* in a very seductive way.

Martino obviously knew this cute young thing. Charlie learned for the first time that Martino could speak and understand Spanish. Later, this was to become very important in their arrest of the speed boats delivering liquor from Cuba.

Martino turned to Charlie and indicated that if it was alright with him, he would go visit this hot little number that night.

Martino walked a little way, and then turned down a side street to Maria's upstairs apartment. Maria greeted Martino with a big hug, a wet kiss, and then wrapped her long beautiful legs around Martino's waist.

Passion, heightened by seeing Martino earlier in the evening, was now more pronounced than ever before. His black curly hair and olive skin made him a real ladies' man.

Maria slipped out of her dress, then her bra, and finally her silk underpants. Of course, this excited Martino, and soon the two were in a hot embrace on the squeaky, four-poster bed.

It was well known (by Martino) that Maria had a cute roommate, but when Charlie was invited to join in a good time, he refused and went back to his room and called it an evening. He sure missed his young wife and two children.

During the next few days, to pass the time while waiting for Garcia to inform the agents of the next rum run, Charlie strolled down to the docks to view the boats and the beautiful green water. On his second day, while watching a big ocean liner dock, a man initiated a conversation with Charlie. The man introduced himself as Ernest Hemingway and said he was just getting ready for a fishing trip out in the Gulf and invited Charlie to join him on his fishing boat.

As neither man knew each other before this meeting, they attempted to get acquainted. Ernest told Charlie that he was an author and journalist. Charlie replied that he was between jobs and just vacationing in the Keys. After all, Charlie did not want to "blow" his cover as a federal agent.

Charlie noticed on the back of Ernest's boat was written in bold letters *Pilor*. Charlie was always curious and asked why his new friend had named his boat the *Pilor*. With a deep laugh, Ernest stated that this was the name of his current wife, Pauline. Ernest's nickname for Pauline was *Pilor*.

Charlie didn't know anything about his new friend, but soon learned that he had written several books and was a well-known author.

Like Charlie, Ernest had dark hair, but he also had a black mustache. Both were big men, and many, mistakenly, could have thought that they were brothers. That is, except for the mustache. The Bureau would not let Charlie grow any extra facial hair even though he was undercover. As you remember, the exception was when Charlie was in West Virginia as an undercover criminal.

Since the night before there had been a storm, the Gulf was a little rough, with the small fishing boat being tossed about in five-foot waves. Needless to say, Charlie, being a landlubber, spent most of the morning hanging over the edge of the boat barfing. Ernest thought that this was pretty funny and would not tell the captain of the boat to return to port until he caught enough fish for Pauline, himself, and the many cats he had at his large home in the heart of Key West. Charlie thought to himself that he had better develop the knack of boating before he ventured out to arrest the smugglers in the Gulf.

Once back on shore, Ernest invited his new friend to join his wife, Pauline, and himself for an evening meal of the grouper he caught on the fishing trip.

Ernest asked Charlie to join him in the kitchen as he cleaned the fish. Through an open window, Ernest would throw the guts of the fish to the waiting cats that seemed to be everywhere on the property.

After dinner, Ernest produced some excellent Jamaican dark rum. Along with a Cuban cigar, the two men enjoyed the evening as Ernest kept Charlie captivated with his stories of being a war correspondent in Spain. The rum was the best that Charlie had ever tasted. Of course, he knew that the consumption of liquor was illegal. However, Charlie was not going to blow his cover, and besides, the rum was delicious.

Later that evening, Charlie stumbled back to his rented room. He couldn't get to sleep as the room seemed to be spinning around and around.

The next morning, after a couple of cups of very strong coffee and a glass of tomato juice, he was able to once again walk a straight line. Everything seemed to be fine, except that the strong sun hurt his eyes, forcing him to buy a cap and pull the bill down over his eyebrows.

There was still no word from Garcia. Charlie needed to check in with Martino, and he had an idea just where to find him.

Martino did not seem to mind that there had been no action for the agents. He had all the action he needed from Maria.

Charlie knocked at Maria's door. As she slowly opened the door, Charlie could see Martino lying on the bed and smoking one of those marijuana cigarettes. He was as bare as a new-born baby. In the meantime, Maria had slipped into a flimsy and very sexy cover-up.

It was now time to search for Garcia. Otherwise, if they couldn't find him, the agents needed to look for another informant.

After an extensive search, they finally found Garcia in a local bar on Whitehall Street, and with a little arm twisting, were able to find out that a shipment of rum would be heading to Key West from Cuba in a couple of days. With the help of the locals at the port, Martino and Charlie rented the fastest speed boat available. The fairly new mahogany speed boat had won numerous races in the area, and this was deemed to be the fastest boat available for the agents. The only concern Charlie had was the expense report that he had to submit to his superiors justifying paying for the rent of the boat. *"Oh hell,"* thought Charlie, *"what if we had to buy the damn boat!"*

Well, one other concern Charlie had was whether or not Martino really had the skill to run the boat. From the beginning of this plan, Martino had boasted that he was an experienced pilot.

Since Martino was a federal agent, he was allowed to legally be in possession of a variety of firearms. He kept these weapons carefully hidden in a back shed of his house. Before the sun was up on the morning of the confiscation of the illegal liquor, they met at Martino's house, and together they chose their weapons for the trip.

Besides the .45 pistols, each man had a "tommy gun." The agents wrapped the tommy guns in blankets that Martino had stored for such an occasion. At that time of the morning, very few pedestrians on the streets noticed the men as they made their way to the boat. The day before, they had taken several jugs of water and various food items to the boat.

Garcia had told them the route the smugglers would be taking from Cuba. He also told them that the Dry Tortugas would be a good place to hide their boat while waiting for the illegal booze. The Dry Tortugas had the distinction of having Fort Jefferson built on this isolated island. During the Civil War, the Union would confiscate goods being sent to the Confederacy in Florida and the Carolinas.

As Fort Jefferson is 70 miles from Key West, it took Martino and Charlie almost a half day to reach the island. As the sun slid beneath the horizon, the two agents made sure their guns were loaded and in good working order.

Both Charlie and Martino were well equipped, as each one had a Thompson submachine gun, M1921. The "tommy gun" shot a .45 slug and was fairly new, as they were first manufactured in 1919. The gangsters in Chicago called this famous gun a "Chicago Typewriter," and they were used by Capone and other criminal elements, as well as the federal agents.

Charlie and Martino hoped that this would be a peaceful arrest. However, they were ready for whatever would take place that evening.

The two agents found a secluded cove on the far side of the island and waited in darkness for the sound of the motor on the rum runners' boat. They knew the boat from Cuba would be running without lights. Therefore, being as quiet as possible, they listened for the propellers of the boat churning the Gulf water.

It was well after midnight when the agents heard, and then sighted, not one, but two boats about a quarter mile from their hideout. Martino asked Charlie if chasing one boat and capturing the criminals would satisfy the agency. Charlie had a plan. He thought that they would chase one boat, and with their "tommy guns," spray a clip of bullets at the water line of the boat and the engine. This would stop one boat dead in the water while they chased the second boat.

The speed of the agents' rented speed boat was all that was needed, as they soon caught up with the first boat. After a spray of bullets that disabled one boat, they chased the second boat and soon caught up with it. With Martino driving the speed boat, Charlie kept his gun on the rum runners, and side-by-side, they raced toward Key West.

With the help of a megaphone, Martino called out to the rum runners, *"Apaguen el motor y arrojen sus armas al agua."* Of course, the Cubans in the boat complied with the request, and after cutting their engine, threw their guns in the water. Charlie was sure glad that Martino could speak Spanish, as this arrest was turning out to be easier than expected.

After escorting the second boat to port in Key West, the agents raced back at full throttle to capture the first boat and arrest the rum runners. As the criminals' boat was damaged, the agents didn't think they would be going anywhere. Their only concern was that with all of the .45 slugs shot into the waterline of the boat, it might sink. After all, they wanted the criminals alive and not eaten by sharks.

Of course, by the time the agents arrived back at the disabled boat, the criminals had thrown the cases of rum in the water and attempted to sink them. Fortunately, the agents were able to retrieve a couple of cases that were floating in the water. The two cases would be sufficient evidence for a conviction.

This time, the agents had to transfer the three criminals to their own boat because the criminals' boat was sinking with the bullet holes just below the water line. Waiting at the port were several more agents and the local police, who escorted the six criminals to the local jail on the island. One federal agent agreed to sit in the jail that night and wait for the rum runners to be escorted to Miami. Charlie still did not trust the local police.

Although Charlie was honest and would not do anything illegal, nor be unfaithful to his wife, he had developed a taste for the good Jamaican rum. Therefore, on the way back to the port in Key West, both Martino and Charlie had placed a couple of bottles of the good rum in their duffel bags and hid them under the seats of the boat. The duffel bags would be retrieved at a more opportune time.

The criminal element in both Key West and Havana still had not identified the two feds who had made the arrest just outside Fort Jefferson. Therefore, both Charlie and Martino were to stay in touch with Garcia and wait for the next "run" from Cuba.

Now, Martino had no trouble waiting for the next assignment as he had Maria for entertainment. However, Charlie had time on his hands with little to do in Key West. As Charlie's new friend, Ernest, had a habit of writing his stories until noon each day, the mornings went very slowly for Charlie, with no special assignments and no other friends.

One very amusing story Ernest told Charlie was that a few weeks before they met for the first time, Pauline had decided they needed a goldfish pond in their back yard. Well, one afternoon, Pauline was walking in front of *Sloppy Joe's Bar* and found that they were remodeling the men's restroom. All six of the urinals were stacked outside on the sidewalk for anyone to take. Of course, the bar served only soft drinks at the time. Pauline then thought that by laying the urinal flat and decorating the edges with colorful tile, this would make a wonderful small goldfish pond. So Pauline carried out her plan, and the unusual goldfish pond remains today.

After hearing this story, Charlie thought to himself, *"Only yesterday, Ernest and I could have been pissing into that urinal."*

In the afternoon, Ernest would often invite Charlie to accompany him on his fishing expeditions. It was then that Charlie soon developed a love for fishing that would carry over into his retirement years.

The only disadvantage of living in Key West was that Charlie never learned to like the taste of fish. As he had grown up in the Midwest, his taste buds were toned for the good beef raised in Iowa and eastern South Dakota. Anyway, Charlie had become deathly sick while eating a tuna sandwich while on wiretap duty in Omaha.

It was to no one's surprise that the only informant that the feds had right there in Key West was Garcia. However, after several weeks with no contact, it seemed that Garcia was nowhere to be found. Without Garcia to tell them of the expected shipments, there was no reason for Charlie and Martino to spend any more time in Key West. Much to the delight of Martino, he was to stay in Key West and try to find another "stool pigeon." In the meantime, Charlie was given a week's vacation to return to Elk Point to reunite with his family.

Chapter 5

Return to Chicago

After learning that Charlie could speak Italian, the agency ordered him to return to Chicago. The Italian speaking Mafia was running the majority of illegal activities in the "Windy City."

Reporting to the Chicago office, Charlie presented himself to his superiors on State Street. The office was in an obscure upstairs flat. Evidently, the Bureau could not afford a nice office like the FBI had in a different part of the city.

Again, due to Charlie's understanding of Italian, he was assigned wiretap duty. As Charlie had a wife and two children to support, he thought it necessary to accept any assignments given to him just to keep his job.

This time, Charlie was to check into a hotel in Cicero. It seems that most of the Mob had located in this suburb just outside Chicago.

His fellow agent on the wiretap was a clean-cut chap by the name of Tony. Tony could also understand a little Italian, as he had been raised in Chicago by his immigrant parents from northern Italy. It is well known that the majority of the Italian Mafia was from Sicily. Therefore, Tony's dialect was noticeable when he spoke to anyone from Sicily. Fortunately, all Tony had to do was listen to the wiretap and not speak with anyone from Sicily. Again, this assignment was boring, and the food provided to the agents was not the best.

Most of the time, the gangsters would not reveal anything of importance, which took place inside the fancy Klas Restaurant located on West Cermak Road. Instead, the men would huddle outside the Italian up-scale restaurant and plan their next activity.

For several weeks, Charlie and Tony positioned themselves in a hotel room across the street from the restaurant. Tony used binoculars to read the lips of the gangsters when they were facing the street. At times, the assembled men had their backs turned, and the agents could not obtain any information. Unfortunately, very little information was obtained from this operation, and the assignment was terminated.

It was in December 1933 that the Twenty-first Amendment to the Constitution was adopted, repealing the Eighteenth Amendment that had outlawed the production and sale of alcoholic beverages. It is probably a little known fact that one reason for the repeal of Prohibition and the Twenty-first Amendment being passed was that in 1933, President Franklin D.

Roosevelt thought that to revive the legitimate alcohol industry would generate thousands of new jobs and would help the economy in the wake of a very bad economy.

With the repeal of the Eighteenth Amendment, Charlie and other agents thought that perhaps they would lose their jobs. Prematurely, Charlie called his wife in Elk Point and said he was coming home, as he thought that any day he would receive word that his services were no longer needed. As fortune would have it, Charlie was wrong on the anticipated termination notice from Washington.

The five New York Mafia families had realized that with the end of Prohibition, they needed to keep the illegal money coming in by continuing with their other illegal activities. Prohibition had enriched the Mafia so well that they had sufficient startup money and enforcement to bankroll new rackets and crimes. Or they could simply take over existing businesses from rival ethnic Jewish and Irish criminals.

It has been reported that Luciano had made at least twelve million dollars from his bootlegging days. This amount was taken in only one year. The year was 1925. However, he had to "pay out" a large sum in expenses, mainly for a small army of truck drivers and guards. Also, he made bribes to law enforcement officials and agents. Even with his large expenses, he is reported to have cleared four million dollars.

Therefore, with the end of Prohibition, the Federal Government had taken note of the fact that the families in New York alone were taking over other illegal activities such as bookmaking, loan-sharking, prostitution, narcotics trafficking, robberies, and cargo hijacking. It was primarily due to the increase of these crimes that the Federal Government put together the Federal Bureau of Investigation in 1935.

Also, the Federal Government formed a new enforcement agency, the Alcohol, Tobacco, and Firearms Agency, or ATF. It was important that now that the consumption of alcohol was legal, the Federal Government collect the taxes imposed on both cigarettes and alcohol.

The Federal Government also wanted to control illegal firearms as much as possible. However, the latter was a daunting task and not very successful, as there were many automatic machine guns in the possession of the criminal element.

The Bureau was going to reorganize, and with Charlie's exemplary record of arrests, he was going to be offered a job as a special agent under the new title of Alcohol, Tobacco, and Firearms. The unit would report to the Treasury Department. Although there would be fewer agents, the ATF would expand into all states and enforce these new regulations.

Charlie's first assignment was to move his family to Minneapolis, Minnesota. By this time, the Campbell family had a new addition to its family. A boy was born, and they called him Calvin.

When this new boy arrived in the Campbell family, Charlie thought his new son was the most perfect baby in the world. Therefore, he called Calvin's older brother and sister to come to the hospital to see their new brother.

Well, Leona arrived with her best friend, Lorna. Calvin was in the arms of his mother, Beulah. After one look at her new baby brother, Leona promptly fainted. As she was falling to the floor, she knocked off the vase of roses that was on the bedside table beside the new mother. Of course, water soaked Beulah's bed, causing the nurse extra duty when she changed the bed linen. This did not make the grouchy nurse very happy.

As there were two beds in the hospital room, Leona was promptly placed in the empty bed near her mother. Of course, this upset Charlie, as he could not understand big sister's reaction. It was years later that Leona told the family that her new brother was *the ugliest baby she had ever seen.*

When the nurse returned with baby Calvin in her arms, she looked at one bed and then the other. The nurse thought to herself, *"Now which one of these ladies is the mother of this brat."*

As the Great Depression of the early 1930s arrived, all families experienced hard times – even those with government checks that arrived with regularity. Although Charlie's salary was somewhat low, the family of five could survive as the two older children were now going to college and working part time.

The Campbells were no exception to the plight of living with meager resources. Beulah enrolled at the University of Minnesota and obtained a provisional teacher's certificate. The course of study took only two years due to the fact that this was all that was required to be a teacher in those days. Although teaching positions were difficult to obtain, Beulah did manage to tutor several children to earn a few dollars for groceries.

Meanwhile, back in Omaha, Bernie had received a promotion and was now a special agent for the ATF.

Charlie's source for confidential information from Bernie's office was Alice Jane. She also suspected that Bernie was "on the payroll" of a Mafia family in Chicago.

Being very careful, Alice Jane would often stay after the office closed and search through Bernie's desk drawers and files in order to send any incriminating information to Charlie. After not receiving letters from Alice Jane for a number of weeks, Charlie inquired as to the whereabouts of his source. The only answer he received was from a "friendly" cab driver and the landlady in Alice Jane's upstairs flat. It was rather strange that after working in Bernie's office for so many years that she would mysteriously move out of town without telling Charlie. The landlady could not supply much information, as Alice Jane had pretty much stayed to herself and did not have any friends who frequented her apartment.

It was not until weeks later that his second informant, a detective in the Omaha police department, reported to Charlie that Alice Jane's body had been found in a landfill outside of Omaha. She had been shot in the back of the head, execution style. This had the earmarks of a Mafia "hit."

From the information that Charlie had gathered over the years, it was now time to turn over all incriminating information related to Bernie's activities to the FBI and let them pursue his possible involvement with the Mafia.

It should be known that the Federal Bureau of Investigation, or FBI, was a newly formed government unit. The new agency's first director was a very ambitious law enforcement professional by the name of J. Edgar Hoover.

As the FBI was put into place in 1935, this would be their first important case. The agents of the FBI were all anxious to resolve this situation pursuing the Italian Mafia. The reason being was that the new agents were recruited from other law enforcement agencies, and all had a strong dislike for the Mafia.

Months later, when Charlie was meeting with FBI officials in Washington, he learned of his own danger, as certain unsavory characters had learned that Alice Jane had been sending him information.

Not only was the incriminating information found concerning Bernie's connection to the Mafia family a reason for Charlie's current danger, but Mr. Hoover told Charlie that during his battle at Key West several months previously, Charlie had critically shot a Mafia family's cousin during the speedboat race.

Therefore, Mr. Hoover thought perhaps Charlie's family had better be relocated under the "witness protection plan." Charlie thought that indeed this would be a good plan for his family, but that he wanted to continue working as an ATF agent. However, perhaps a relocation to a more remote location could be a good idea. In this way, he could keep his job and still protect his family. After all, Charlie's family meant a lot to him, and he sure didn't want any harm to come to them due to his own actions in tracing down corruption.

Chapter 6

Witness Protection

Charlie received a week's leave to move his family to Rapid City, South Dakota. This was about as far as the family agreed to move.

Charlie stayed in Minneapolis and continued to work with two other agents to investigate illegal liquor production. The three men were responsible for the state of Minnesota and parts of both Iowa and eastern South Dakota.

Using an informant, Charlie learned that in the woodlands of northern Minnesota, there was suspicious activity, as trucks, usually not seen in the area, were traveling on the back roads near Hibbing and Chisholm. The thick woods located in the Mesabi Iron Range would be an ideal location to set up a set of stills. In addition, a group of strangers had been seen in grocery stores buying sugar. Another group of men had inquired about where they could buy some copper tubing and wooden barrels.

Again, Charlie would need to adapt to the location and take on the role of one of the locals. If he wore his typical three-piece suit, he would stand out as a fed. Therefore, he posed as a drifter passing through the area looking for a job. To look more like the locals, Charlie grew a beard and bought some wool shirts and heavy cotton pants. Through a friend, he borrowed a pair of well-worn boots.

The Bureau found a used, "beat up" car for Charlie to travel to the location of the suspected still. If there ever was need for a car chase, this dilapidated car certainly would not be able to catch even a slow moving horse!

It would be dangerous for Charlie to travel the back roads, as he might accidently run across the still. Instead, he obtained a job as a mechanic in Hibbing.

Just as he had done in West Virginia, he would frequent the local bars and establish a relationship with the locals. The difference now was that he could order his favorite drink, a boilermaker. This is a shot of whiskey, followed by a slug of beer. Charlie's favorite whiskey was Jim Beam.

Strandburg's Garage and Towing was the only place for the locals to have their cars repaired. Mr. Melvin Strandburg also had an old tow truck that was used to pull cars and logging trucks out of the mud on the back roads. Of course, Charlie volunteered to drive the tow truck in order to venture out into the countryside.

However, during this particular summer, there were not as many calls to the garage.

After consulting the main office in St. Paul, the best plan was for Charlie and the two other agents to wait until hunting season and then pose as deer hunters and try to find the stills. It was rumored that Charlie had the best nose in smelling the whiffs of sour mash that was used in making the moonshine.

Sure enough, on one foggy morning, as the three hunters were leaving their cabin and filing into the forest for the hunt, Charlie caught the smell of sour mash coming from the north. It was decided that they would travel away from this location and travel south. The agents' plan was to wait until the middle of the night and to venture north to determine if they could find the bootleggers' illegal still.

With the help of the state police and the local sheriff, there were five law enforcement officers, each carrying a .30 caliber hunting rifle and a side arm of their trusted .38 revolver.

Luck would have it that there were only three bootleggers on the site. After a surprise attack and the easy arrest, the agents destroyed the large barrels of moonshine.

Somehow, the local newspaper in Hibbing had caught wind of the arrest and was waiting at the local jail in the morning as the agents brought the criminals into town.

This rather large operation was the only action that had taken place that year. Therefore, Charlie was able to take some time off and rejoin his family in Rapid City.

* * * * *

Charlie's oldest son, Edward Eugene, had obtained employment in the Black Hills in the CCC, or Civilian Conservation Corps. Unlike his father, Ed had auburn, wavy hair and was somewhat slight in build. However, with the physical labor demanded of the young men working in the Black Hills, Ed was in great physical condition.

One noticeable positive characteristic that Ed had that had eluded his father was his sense of humor. He was always telling jokes and pulling pranks on his supervisor and the other boys in the camp. Due to his fun-loving characteristics, all of the boys in the camp really liked him and would seek out his company.

Ed would often go AWOL from the campsite to sneak into Hill City to attend dances with the local girls. As none of the boys in the camp had cars, they would stand on the highway and attempt to get to Hill City by hitchhiking. At this period in our history, more people were trusting and would pick up the boys for the short ride to Hill City.

Now, without a car to take the girls out and have a little smooching, etc., the boys would persuade the girls to walk a little way into the woods behind the high school where the dances were held. Now, if you wonder how they managed to sneak back into camp late in the night, well, you will just have to ask my big brother Ed.

Meanwhile, back at the camp, the work was back-breaking, as the young men, all in their teens and early twenties, were building rest areas and clearing dead pine left over from the winter.

* * * * *

Sometimes the Mafia can be very vicious and "go after" an informant's family. This was the case when the gang in Chicago found out that Charlie's son was working in the Black Hills of South Dakota.

After a long car trip from Chicago, a couple of "hit men" arrived in Rapid City about midnight one summer evening. After renting a cabin at Bacon Park campground on the edge of Rapid City, they asked the manager where the CCC boys were working. It was strange that a couple of men with black suits would want to know the location of the workers. Deliberately, the manager stated he thought the boys were in the northern hills around Sturgis.

The "hit men" from Chicago were not fooled by this tale, and instead drove south out of Rapid City until they found the CCC camp of neatly arranged cabins near Hill City. The two thugs from Chicago thought that this would be an easy "hit." What can a group of unarmed young men do to stop the likes of them?

Little did the boys from Chicago know that the cabin manager was a friend of the CCC supervisor. After a phone call from the cabin manager, the supervisor had one of their own stay up each night and watch for anything suspicious.

At about three one morning, the two thugs stopped their big Packard about one mile from the camp, and with each one carrying a sawed-off shotgun, very quietly approached the cabins.

The director of the Civilian Conservation Corps selected "Little John" to stand guard most nights. Now, John was anything but small. Standing over six foot seven with broad shoulders and a barrel of a chest, he was a formidable young man. Actually, he was more a boy than a man. In fact, he had a reputation of chopping down a young pine sapling tree with one swing with only his left arm.

Anyway, none of the other boys would tease John. Although large in size, he could not take the teasing and would often verbally explode without any reason. The director had to tread softly when assigning jobs, as he did not want to upset John.

I suppose today a psychologist would label John with some type of abnormal condition. In fact, he probably would not be allowed to have any type of weapon, even though at times he may have needed one.

Armed with only a double-edge, and very sharp axe, John stood guard the night the men from Chicago arrived. When he first sighted the two strangers, he snuck up behind the men, and with a mighty sideward swing, knocked the first would-be assassin to the ground. The second thug swung his shotgun around and managed a single shot that only grazed the right arm of John. With only his left arm mobile, John was able to swing the axe and catch the assassin square in the gut. With a mighty yell, the killer fell to the ground seriously wounded.

With all the yelling, the boys piled out of their cabins to find out what was happening. Alvin, the director of the CCC group, would not let the boys view the bodies of the maimed gangsters, as it was not a pretty sight. The second hit man's guts were spilled on the pine-covered ground, with blood splattered on the nearest cabin wall. The first assassin was on the ground, still unconscious, with his head wound still bleeding. Of course, blood was all over the ground and had spread for nearly two feet around the wounded men.

The highway patrol and an ambulance from Rapid City were called to clean up the mess at the camp and then to take the two injured men to the St. John's Hospital in Rapid City. Immediately, a city policeman was placed outside the room of each wounded man to protect him from local friends of the Campbell family who might want to take the law into their own hands. Also, there was the danger that some of the Mafia brothers from Chicago would pay a visit to silence the patients before they would be forced to divulge any information about the current plan to destroy Charlie Campbell and his family. Later that first night, the man with the stomach wound died.

The Mafia had failed in an assassination attempt on one of Charlie's family members. But the danger continued for several months.

Chapter 7

The Trial of Little John

The attempted attack at the CCC camp and the killing of one of the attackers by Little John resulted in him being arrested. After a short trial, he was found not guilty of murder and exonerated of the other charge of attempted assault with a deadly weapon.

Little John's brave activities that night brought him much attention in the Black Hills. Several times during the next few years, he was called upon to provide security when groups or individuals needed protection.

When the Mafia's Supreme Council found out that it was Dutch Schultz (a leading criminal not attached to the Italian families) who had targeted the Campbell family, they were furious. Why? Because it was an unwritten law that the Mob was not to target law enforcement. Anyway, this was the rule of the Italian Mafia families.

The Mafia Supreme Council unanimously vetoed Schultz's targeting of Agent Campbell and his family. However, it was Dutch's rum being run from Cuba. Also, it was Dutch Schultz's cousin who was shot by Charlie in the boat race outside Key West.

Schultz's gang was the only non-Italian organization left to operate in New York that was not subservient to the Mafia. Underworld cognoscenti referred to the five Costa Nostra families and Schultz's outfit as "The Big Six."

Being an astute businessman and somewhat fearing the Mafia, Schultz called off the assignation attempts on the Campbell family.

Later it was learned that Joseph Bonanno was heard to say the plot was insane, and Schultz needed to have a muzzle placed on him.

The reasoning behind the Mafia's policy against targeting lawmen was that this would unleash enormous public outcry against the rackets.

Therefore, it was through informants inside the criminal element that Charlie learned that the "hit" had been taken off his family.

Chapter 8

The Peaceful Years

Now stationed in Rapid City, Charlie Campbell shared an office with the local FBI agent. Together, they shared one secretary in a very cramped and sparse office upstairs above the local United States Post Office.

As Charlie had not graduated from high school, he was embarrassed to give his mandatory weekly reports to the shared secretary for typing. The reports needed to be sent to the St. Paul district office each Sunday evening. The large envelope would be placed in the mail car in Rapid City to be delivered to St. Paul the next morning. Rather, it was Beulah, his always supportive wife, who would type the report on Sunday afternoon. Their son, Calvin, would then ride his bicycle to the train station to place the very valuable document in the slot of the mail car.

Charlie was given a government car to patrol his territory, which included the entire western half of

South Dakota. The territory extended from the Missouri River to the Wyoming border. Also, he patrolled from the North Dakota border to the Nebraska border.

This period of time in the late 1930s and early 1940s was relatively peaceful, with no major "stills" found in the Black Hills or on the barren prairies of western South Dakota. Nevertheless, Charlie needed to travel the entire territory from Monday morning until Friday afternoon. His primary duty was to check that the numerous small-town bars had an updated tax certificate displayed above the bar.

Charlie also would check grocery stores and hardware stores to see if anyone had purchased an unusual quantity of sugar. In the hardware stores, he checked to see if anyone had purchased a large supply of copper tubing. Both sugar and copper were necessary to produce "moonshine."

* * * * *

After both World War II and the Korean Conflict, the soldiers would often gather automatic weapons left behind by the retreating enemy. It was the law in the early 1940s that citizens could not own weapons that could spray a full clip of bullets in a split second. However, many G.I.'s would disassemble their weapons, and piece by piece, ship the pieces to their homes in the United States, planning to keep them as war souvenirs.

Now, Charlie's relationship with the veterans of South Dakota was extremely "tight," as they all knew that his son, Ed, had served in Europe during World War II. Therefore, for the most part, the veterans would surrender their assembled weapons to Charlie.

Now, Charlie had received orders to take the weapons back to Rapid City and have the firing pin removed and place a lead slug in the barrel. In this way, the weapon could not be fired. On his next road trip to a designated location, he would return the weapon to the veteran.

As a tourist, if you drive the back roads of South Dakota, and happen to stop at a rural tavern, you more than likely will see a small tri-pod machine gun sitting on a ledge behind the bar.

Calvin still remembers waiting on Friday afternoon for his father to return from his road trip and running to the car to see how many automatic weapons were collected during the week.

Now, Calvin was not allowed to play with the guns outside. But this did not prevent him from lying on the floor in the house and pretending to shoot the weapon. Charlie considered this safe for his son since bullets for the guns were not available.

On Monday morning, the weapons would disappear as the local gunsmith would perform the necessary alterations to the machine guns.

This assignment in Rapid City was a somewhat easy time for Charlie. He enjoyed his time with his family and the opportunity to fish in the many streams and lakes in the Black Hills. But this assignment soon came to an end.

Chapter 9

The Canadian Connection

Although Charlie's time in Rapid City was primarily peaceful, he still had to be on the lookout for any illegal activities. Therefore, as he had done in other locations, he relied on informants to notify him of any criminal activities. Sometimes, these informants had useful information, and at other times, they were only looking for a "handout" and really didn't have anything useful to warrant an arrest.

It was on a cold, wintery evening that the Campbells' doorbell rang, and Charlie put on his overcoat to talk with this gentleman on the porch. Charlie would never let an informant enter his home, as many of these individuals had criminal records and could not be trusted around his family.

On this particular night, the informant did have some very useful information. It seemed that the taxi cabs in Rapid City were selling untaxed scotch whiskey.

Now Charlie had to act to catch whoever was behind this very profitable endeavor.

As Charlie was a well-known law enforcement officer in Rapid City, he could not work undercover in this case. He needed to call an agent from St. Paul to act as a customer and buy the illegal scotch.

It was the next morning that Charlie made the call from his office and informed his superiors of the situation. Of course, with due haste, the agent from St. Paul made the drive to Rapid City to assist in the arrest.

It was important that the federal agents not only arrest the cab drivers, but also find out the ring leader behind this scheme.

Weeks passed, and the agents were stumped as to how the scotch was finding its way to Rapid City. Finally, a bartender in a bar directly across the street from the agents' office called and asked to meet Charlie at midnight in an alley in back of the nightclub.

This bartender usually took a "smoke break" outside about midnight, and therefore, his absence was not noticed by his boss. Of course, the bartender wanted a payout to inform on his boss. However, Charlie was not given any more money to pay informants. Therefore, he took from his overcoat pocket a device called a "come along." A "come along" looks like a single handcuff, but with a handle that would twist the wrist of the victim. Grabbing the wrist of the bartender, Charlie twisted until information was readily produced. It was luck that nobody heard the bartender yelling with pain as

Charlie tightened the grip of this device. The information was that the scotch was stored in the basement of the bar. The bartender called Charlie a "son-of-a-bitch" as he went back to work.

With the assistance of the agent from St. Paul, the South Dakota State Police, and the local police, a raid on the bar was made the next night. The confiscation of the scotch was helpful. However, now the agents needed to know the "ring leader" behind this operation.

With the local newspaper sworn to secrecy by the police, none of the activities of the arrest was reported. It was as if nothing out of the ordinary had happened, and the cab drivers were allowed to continue their selling of the scotch.

It was important to find out the Canadian source and the organization behind this brazen scheme. The decision was made that the agent from St. Paul would attempt to stand on the highway and hitchhike back to Canada. He would flag down only trucks that seemed capable of carrying large cases of scotch.

As luck would have it, the truck driver who had just delivered a shipment of scotch to Rapid City was driving back to Canada with an empty truck. His route home took him north from Rapid City and over the border into North Dakota. The driver's whereabouts was phoned to an agent in St. Paul.

Doug, the agent from St. Paul who had been waiting for this alert, drove to a truck stop just across the South Dakota boarder into North Dakota. Drinking coffee at the run-down diner and dressed like a down-

and-out drifter, he appeared to be hoping for a ride to the North Dakota oil fields looking for work. He identified the truck and approached the truck driver who had delivered the last shipment to Rapid City and asked, no begged, for a ride to Williston to apply for a job.

By the time the truck neared Williston, North Dakota, another ATF agent by the name of Steven was in place at a truck stop, which was the first one on the highway just before entering the city. When the truck pulled into the truck stop, Doug thanked the driver for getting him to Williston. Little did the Canadian driver know that yet another agent was about to take over surveillance and hop a ride into Canada. This time the driver was a little wary of having another "dead-beat" passenger riding with him into Canada. However, Steven was very persuasive and even agreed to pay the truck driver twenty dollars for the ride.

The truck driver wanted to know where Steven wanted to go in Canada. Of course, Steven wanted to go to meet the driver's boss. But Steven had to come up with a story allowing him to stay in the truck until they arrived at the town in Canada where the stash of scotch was being loaded.

Now came the hard part. Steven convinced the truck driver that he was "on the run" from authorities in North Dakota, as he had just robbed a bank. Steven even showed the driver the pistol he used in the heist.

It was even more important now that the driver lose this hitchhiker. However, greed took over as Steven pushed a $100 bill into the driver's shirt pocket, and with a pistol in his right hand, the driver thought, *"What the hell, what choice do I have now?"*

The driver stated that he needed to turn in his truck at Brandon, Manitoba. Steven tricked the nervous driver into revealing where the truck terminal was located in the city and the name of the dispatcher on duty at the terminal. This was enough information for Steven, and he directed the driver to let him off at the next intersection so that he could thumb a ride to Winnipeg.

Now that the federal agency knew where the trucks were loading the scotch, the next step was for a third agent to obtain employment at the terminal in Brandon to find out more about who was directing the entire operation. The third agent's name was Alex. This agent's job was to apply for work at the terminal. Alex was an experienced, over-the-road, eighteen wheeler truck driver. After dressing the part, Alex presented himself to the dispatcher and asked for a job driving.

The dispatcher was in need of drivers as business was brisk. Therefore, when Alex produced his papers certifying him as a licensed driver for big rigs, he was immediately given the job.

As all trucks were on the road, except for the one just returning from South Dakota, Alex had time to work in the warehouse. One especially dark night, at about three in the morning, Alex broke into the terminal and began searching the office files in hopes of finding names that would incriminate the "ring leader" of the entire operation.

Well, Alex was unsuccessful in finding any helpful information, so it was back to square one.

Not to give up, the supervisor of agents at the St. Paul office had yet another plan. Alex was to wait a couple of nights, or until the next night when there was no moon, and break into the terminal and torch the building – scotch and all. The idea was to find out if the terminal, with all that liquor, had an owner who would file for the insurance to cover his loss. By finding the owner, the case could come to a close, and the clever operation would be shut down.

Sure enough, Alex was successful in starting a fire which lasted most of the night. The owner, a Mr. Cramer Osgood, filed for insurance two days later to cover the loss of his building.

It was now time to turn over the case to the Royal Canadian Police. Of course, the United States Government would never admit to starting the fire that consumed the warehouse where the scotch was being stored. Sometimes, clandestine operations are necessary to see that justice is served. As the United States started involving itself in more complex operations during the Cold War with Russia, more of these incidents began to occur.

Needless to say, Charlie Campbell received a commendation for his role in first discovering and then arresting the local distributors. It was now time to release all of the information to the *Rapid City Journal*.

Of course, Agent Campbell's picture was on the front page of the paper. As Rapid City had only a population of about 40,000 at the time, many residents knew of the Campbell family.

Chapter 10

The North Star Raid

It is a well-known fact that most law enforcement agencies work together in a cooperative way. At least that was the norm in the 1950s when Charlie was an agent in Rapid City.

When Charlie decided that it was not necessary to travel the country roads or visit the scattered little towns in western South Dakota, he would often visit his friends at the local police station. Together, they would drink coffee, and on lucky days, have a doughnut that one of the officers would bring to the station. The local police would welcome Charlie as one of their own. This rapport was built, in part, by Charlie often furnishing homemade cinnamon rolls that his talented wife, Beulah, would bake the afternoon before his visit.

On Saturdays, Charlie would often bring his son, Calvin, to the station. On one such Saturday morning visit, Charlie motioned Calvin to the back of the station to see the holding cells. Charlie instructed Calvin to enter a jail cell to experience what it was like to be a criminal and stay in those confined spaces up to 24 hours per day. Calvin really didn't like the idea, especially after his father closed the door of the cell. When the officers in the front asked why Charlie had played this trick on his son, Charlie answered with a knowing smile and stated that, *"I wanted my son to feel the terror of being in jail, and then he would not want to get into any trouble as he approached his teenage years."*

Needless to say, Calvin never forgot the experience and never got into any trouble of any kind. In fact, Calvin was a model student who participated in athletics at Rapid City Central High School, and later enrolled at the University of South Dakota on a scholarship.

It was on one of the Saturday visits that the officers were all in the Chief's office, and Charlie instinctively knew that something was brewing. Well, an informant for the local police had reported that there was gambling at the North Star Bar and Lounge between Rapid City and Sturgis.

In the early 1950s, gambling was illegal in South Dakota, and although not a federal crime, nevertheless, the local police could use all the help possible to shut down this illegal operation. The Chief had already contacted the South Dakota Highway Patrol and the county sheriff. This operation would be a coordinated operation with all participating law enforcement agencies involved.

Now, neither the FBI nor the ATF was supposed to participate, as the law against gambling was not a federal offense. In fact, if Charlie's superiors had found out that Charlie was going to "lend a hand," they would have quickly rejected his participation. However, Charlie liked the "boys" at the station, and as his job had become somewhat boring, welcomed some action.

Therefore, Charlie first called Beulah and told her not to prepare supper for him that night, that he was going to assist the local police in a minor operation. In fact, he asked her if he could invite a few of the "boys" over for pie and coffee after the raid on a nightclub. Now, Charlie did not reveal the name of the establishment, as someone might be listening on the party line.

A little before midnight, a number of cars drove out of Rapid City and headed toward Sturgis. Charlie rode with the local sheriff, as taking his government car on an unauthorized sting would not be approved. However, he did wear his .38 special in his shoulder holster. Unlike most days on the road, this time he did load bullets into the chambers.

After arriving at the North Star and covering all exits, the arrest went very peacefully, and the owners cooperated with all that was asked of them. They really had very little choice when confronted with so many armed law enforcement officers.

The raid was a complete surprise, and the officers collected enough evidence that the District Attorney would not have any difficulty in making a conviction and imposing a large fine, and perhaps jail time, for the owners of this establishment.

As promised, Charlie invited his fellow officers to his home on Columbus Street in Rapid City so they could have coffee and Beulah's delicious apple pie. The neighbors were not upset by the number of police cars at the Campbell home, as they all knew that he was an ATF agent. They probably thought that something **REALLY BIG** was taking place.

Now, most of the evidence had been turned over to the lawyers that night so they could make their case stand up in court. However, a few policemen had taken dice from the North Star and began to play in the front room of Campbell's home.

As Calvin was interested in what was taking place in the living room below, he stood at the top of the stairs and witnessed this action from the upstairs banister. He could see that the cubes were bright red with a gold star on one side. Of course, his mother caught him peeking from the upstairs staircase and promptly sent him to his room, as it was now well past midnight and his bedtime.

In addition to the pie and coffee, a few agents had taken a bottle or two of whiskey and were enjoying a few shots as a follow-up to the pie and coffee.

Now, before Calvin was to walk to school the next morning, both his mother and father told him not to talk about what had happened the night before. For one thing, Charlie was not authorized to have been on the raid. The second reason was that the *Rapid City Journal* was to give some of the details of the raid, and not some runny nose kid at a local school.

Chapter 11

The Sand Hills of Nebraska

It was only a week after the North Star raid that Charlie received an urgent telegram from St. Paul. Evidently, a federal agent had found evidence of a bootleg operation in the desolate sand hills of Nebraska. The assignment to investigate, find, arrest, and destroy any illegal bootleg whiskey was now a priority in this district.

It would be a difficult operation as western Nebraska is a very isolated part of the state. As it is in South Dakota, most of the state's population resides in the eastern part of the state.

Since none of the residents living in the area had ever seen Charlie Campbell, it would be safe for Charlie to once again go "undercover" and blend in with the locals. This time he was to dress the part of an out-of-work drifter with limited skills in both speech and action.

Charlie wondered why he couldn't again assume the role of a car mechanic. The St. Paul office had no reply for Charlie's request and told him to act somewhat mentally limited so that he could hang around the bars and pick up any gossip about illegal activities.

He soon applied for the job of janitor at the only bar in Marsland. The job was very demeaning for Charlie, as he had to clean the toilets and take the abuse that the locals heaped on him because of this supposedly limited mental capacity.

After a few days, nobody paid any attention to the fumbling village idiot. This meant that Charlie could pick up conversations, as nobody suspected that he was a threat of any kind. It was as if he were invisible. This time the authorities in St. Paul were right in selecting the role for him to play.

One evening, as Charlie was inside a toilet stall cleaning the bowl, two locals entered the small room and were discussing the movement of their "hooch" from the area of the still, near the Box Butte Dam to Chadron and Alliance. With this information, Charlie had a better understanding of where the still might be located.

Another plan that was hatched by the agents in St. Paul was that a couple of their men rent a piper cub airplane for a sightseeing adventure that would take them over the Box Butte Dam area. One agent would pilot the plane while the other agent trained his binoculars on the ground below. Sure enough, the agent with the binoculars spotted a large truck leaving a dust trail on a road leading away from the Dam.

It was now time for several agents to change to their cars and drive to the last reported sighting of the fast-moving truck. As luck would have it, a truck approaching the location of the still led the federal cars directly to the site where the bootleg liquor was being made.

It was an easy "bust" to find the still and destroy the illegal "booze." However, the agents' job was not complete.

Through a bit of perhaps illegal, but persuasive, interrogation, it was learned that the illegal jars of moonshine were being stored in the numerous ranches dotting the area. It was necessary to obtain a court order to search the private property of the ranchers. However, the officials in Nebraska were cooperative, and soon the agents were driving to the targeted ranches scattered across the barren landscape of the sand hills of Nebraska.

Charlie was with two other agents when they drove into the dirt-covered yard of a local rancher. Charlie thought that perhaps the best place to hide the "hooch" was the storm cellar about thirty feet from the main house. Each rancher in this barren part of Nebraska had a storm cellar to keep both butter and milk cool and to use to escape in case they sighted a tornado.

With his .38 pistol drawn, Charlie entered the storm cellar. Now, there were no two-legged villains. However, he heard a familiar rattle that he instinctively knew was a rattlesnake. The "rattler" caught Charlie on the upper arm. With his other arm, Charlie caught the four-foot rattler and threw the snake across the darkened room.

One of the agents behind Charlie, by the name of Lewis, witnessed the danger and immediately drew his .38 pistol from his side holster and blasted the rattler.

Charlie thought, *"Now Beulah is really going to be mad, as I volunteered for this assignment and could have bypassed going to Nebraska by faking duties that needed to be performed in South Dakota."*

This rancher happened to be clean, and no moonshine was found on his property. The other agents performed as much first aid on Charlie's arm as they knew how from their limited experience in such situations. It was now time to load Charlie into the car and make a run for the nearest hospital.

The rancher explained that perhaps Chadron was the closest hospital, and so racing along the bumpy and rut-filled, rural roads, the agents made it to the emergency entrance to the Chadron Hospital. Charlie's hand and arm were greatly swollen, and he was in a lot of pain.

Immediately, emergency procedures were performed. The ER doctor had treated many snake bites and knew exactly what to do.

The two agents waiting in the lounge flipped a coin to determine who was going to call Beulah. Well, Ralph lost the coin toss and found a pay phone to make the call.

Beulah, of course, was upset, but also relieved to know that her husband had not been shot by the bootleggers.

The doctor told the agents and Charlie that he had better stay in the hospital a couple of days to watch and see if the swelling and infection were under control.

In the meantime, the agents did find the illegal moonshine in several of the ranchers' storm cellars. If it had not been for Charlie listening to the characters in the bar's restroom, the case may never have been closed. Of course, Charlie hoped that he would never again have to pose as a janitor. Sometimes, the role of a "government man" was not that glamorous!

Chapter 12

Illegal Hooch: Close to Home

Of course, after Charlie recovered from his snake bite and returned home, his family was glad to see him and was relieved to see that he was the same old Charlie, full of wisecracks about his adventures.

The routine continued as Charlie would travel his territory in western South Dakota, and nothing really changed at home. After all, the Prohibition days were over, and the profit in making moonshine was not all that great.

As it is today, many individuals made their own beer or wine. This was not a problem if they did not' attempt to sell the homebrew to make a profit and avoid paying the federal tax.

By 1947, many servicemen were returning from the war and had difficulty in obtaining a well-paid job. Those men whose wives found employment would take advantage of the G.I. Bill that helped pay expenses so they could either return to college or begin college as a freshman.

Many very successful men today received a "boot up" by obtaining their college education and launching into lucrative positions in large corporations, law, or a profession in the medical field. This was all made possible by the assistance the United States Government gave our G.I.'s.

However, there are always individuals who are looking for a "fast buck," and instead of working for a living, would rather indulge in illegal activities, hoping for huge profits. This was the case when an informant appeared at the Campbell residence on Columbus Street. This "seedy" character had reported that he had a friend who had obtained a case of homebrew and some "white lightning" from a home on West Boulevard.

At first, Charlie dismissed this information as just another attempt to get a few bucks for information that might not be totally accurate. After all, West Boulevard was where the upper-middle class resided. But being a conscientious law enforcement agent, it was Charlie's duty to check on the accuracy of the informant's information.

The next morning, as Charlie was having coffee and doughnuts at the local police station, a young recruit, who happened to be a war veteran, strolled by with a hardy greeting. Charlie, looking at the Chief, thought, *"This must be the new recruit they were telling me about. The Department must have known that Thomas would be a very fine addition to the force.*" Now, Thomas was a handsome young lad with crew cut blond hair and a very fine physique.

Charlie was always one step ahead of others, as this gave him a plan on how to check the rumor of booze being sold on West Boulevard.

Now, the Chief of Police owed Charlie for not only his assistance in the raid on the North Star, but also the fine hospitality at Charlie's home after the raid.

Charlie thought that Thomas would be the ideal man to attempt to buy a case of homebrew and a little of the whiskey that reportedly was being sold in town.

Well, Thomas was to wear his old Army field jacket and appear to be having a drinking problem, with little cash to spend on his developed habit of drinking.

One night, after his third drink at a popular bar on Main Street, Thomas was approached by two men who told him that they knew where he could get some cheap homebrew if he would follow them to a nice home on West Boulevard. At the house, Thomas was able to make a purchase, and, therefore obtain the evidence that Charlie needed. Thomas returned the purchased liquor to the local police station where it was stored for the night. Now, there was enough evidence to make the arrest.

The next morning, Charlie called the district office in St. Paul for additional agents to help in making the bust. Although Charlie had helped with the North Star raid, this latest bust was not exactly protocol, as the local police were not to be involved, because making moonshine was a federal offense.

The evening train carried two additional agents from St. Paul, and together they planned on how to seize the operation without anyone getting hurt. With a search warrant in hand, they appeared about midnight at the up-scale residence on West Boulevard. One agent covered the back door, while Charlie and the other agent knocked at the front door, pretending to be customers. Once the chain lock was released, the agents forced themselves into the home and presented the warrant. However, there was no sign of any illegal booze. In fact, it seemed that only a middle-aged man and his wife were present in the large, three-story mansion.

Perhaps the cunning criminals had an informant in the local police department who had given them a warning. The agents could smell the remnants of the alcohol as they moved from room to room. However, after an extensive search of the home from attic to the basement, the agents were about to leave when one of the men put his hand on the banister leading upstairs. Underneath the wooden banister was placed large rubber tubing. By following the tubing, the agents found that it led to the back wall of the attic.

The tubing then went under the wall. Of course, there was a false wall, and after knocking down the plywood panels, another room emerged that contained all of the necessary equipment for their operation. The tubing that ran downstairs was to force the beer to a downstairs parlor where the brew was disbursed. These criminals were perhaps the most clever in hiding their operation that Charlie had ever witnessed.

Now, this was not the end of this story. It seems that in addition to selling liquor, the master criminals had a number of prostitutes who were available for their customers. As suspected, there must have been a snitch who had informed the criminals on the West Boulevard location, as none of the girls were to be seen the night of the raid.

Of course, the city police, sheriff, and state police would now become involved in the case. Although selling moonshine without a license was a federal offense, the presence of prostitutes became the business of a number of police jurisdictions.

After obtaining the necessary papers from the District Attorney, the arrests were made, and the owners of the establishment were cooperative in naming the girls who had been hired.

Perhaps it was a good idea that there was a snitch to inform the owners, as it was possible, *just possible,* that a number of respectable gentlemen would have been present in the home if an arrest had been made the night of the first raid. The arrest made the front page of the *Rapid City Journal.* But think what the headlines would have been if a few community leaders had been caught inside the large home on West Boulevard.

After the case was closed and Charlie was having his usual coffee and doughnuts at the police station, Thomas was coming off the night patrol. Boy, did the assembled officers give him the "raspberries." It seemed as if Thomas had stayed at the residence on West Boulevard for a very extended time.

Now this was still not the end of this story. It seems that Thomas had taken a liking to one of the girls in the establishment on West Boulevard. Sue Ellen was a striking blond with rather large breasts and a very sweet personality. Thomas just couldn't help his feelings for Sue Ellen. During one visit, prior to the arrests of the owners of the brothel, Thomas asked where Sue Ellen lived so that he could continue the relationship.

Sue Ellen had an upstairs apartment downtown on Main Street. She also liked this "hunk" of a policeman, and so very soon, a true romance developed. Thomas asked that Sue Ellen keep their relationship a secret, as his fellow officers would not understand why a nice looking chap like himself would fall head-over-heels for a prostitute.

Now, Thomas was not as innocent as his fellow officers had thought, as he had been stationed in Germany while in the Army and had frequented brothels just outside his base.

The two lovebirds continued their relationship for several months. It wasn't until one evening when Thomas finished his patrol and had checked out for the evening that he had intended to visit Sue Ellen. After climbing the stairs to the apartment, he rang the doorbell and received no response. As Thomas was anxious to see his lover, he began to pound on the door. The next door neighbor heard the loud pounding on the door and went into the hallway to find out what the commotion was all about.

The neighbor told Thomas that a couple of men had arrived at Sue Ellen's door about midnight, and later she was seen in the company of the two middle-aged men leaving with a suitcase and little else.

This would not be the end of the story for Thomas. It seemed that he could not get Sue Ellen out of his mind. It was strange that in Germany he had never really fallen in love with any of the girls with whom he had relations.

Thomas was very discreet in attempting to find where Sue Ellen had disappeared to in the middle of the night. Now, how could Thomas find the whereabouts of his lost love?

One evening he went back to Sue Ellen's former one-bedroom apartment in an attempt to find some source of evidence that would tell him a little more about this mysterious "lady." As the apartment had not been rented yet to someone else, Thomas convinced the landlord to open the door to Sue Ellen's residence so he could search the unit to perhaps learn where she might be, or where her hometown was located.

Thomas indeed found information from a few letters that she had left behind in her haste to leave Rapid City. In her unmailed letters to her brother living in Elgin, Illinois, she admitted that she had been involved in prostitution in Chicago and was the favorite of Dominick "Quiet Dom" Cirillo, a "made" member of the Mafia. This was enough evidence to scare-off

Thomas, who tearfully walked out of the apartment and down Main Street for an hour, before catching a taxi and going home.

Chapter 13

Trouble at the Pine Ridge Indian Reservation

Charlie had no real problems with the Indians on the Pine Ridge Indian Reservation located in the far southwest corner of South Dakota. The Bureau of Indian Affairs had the duty to enforce and oversee the federal laws on Indian reservations.

In fact, Charlie had no difficulty with the Oglala Sioux Tribe living on the reservation until a year before his retirement on June 30, 1954.

The reason was that Congress had passed a law in 1832 that banned the sale of alcohol to Native Americans. However, Dwight D. Eisenhower endorsed public law 277 in 1953 that ended this regulation. The amended law now gave Native American tribes the option of either permitting, or banning, alcohol sales and consumption on their lands.

Many tribes chose to exclude alcohol from their reservations because consumption of alcohol caused serious problems for its people. The Pine Ridge Reservation was one of the Indian reservations that continued the ban on sale and consumption.

Today, 200 of the 293 reservations in the 48 contiguous states have banned alcohol sales in their territories.

Although there were Bureau of Indian Affairs officers, and also tribal police who were responsible to enforce the ban on alcohol, the St. Paul district office called Charlie to travel to Pine Ridge and meet with the law enforcement officers in the area. It seems that the officers of the BIA and tribal police were having a difficult time in enforcing the law. Enterprising distributors of alcohol were making truck runs into the Pine Ridge Reservation at night and depositing their beer and other spirits to cafes, and also to individual homes. From the scattered homes, the locals would purchase the spirits and distribute them to their friends. This was going to be a difficult case to solve as there were no "friendlies" who could be counted on to give the agents any useful information as to where to raid the homes of the residents who were making the illegal purchases.

The only solution to this growing problem was to establish road blocks so that the trucks distributing the alcohol could be stopped and the drivers arrested before their arrival at their destination.

Although the distributors were legitimate alcohol vendors, many of them became greedy and saw a way to make some additional cash. Well, after a number of arrests and the imposing of substantial fines to the distributors, the problem was resolved, and there ceased to be a problem.

Now the Indians still obtained their alcohol. However, it was more difficult, as they had to travel off the reservation to buy the spirits.

After serving on the road blocks for about a month, and then later appearing in court to testify against the distributors, it was time for Charlie to take a much needed vacation. After doing a few repair jobs on his home on Columbus Street and planting his annual garden, Charlie thought that he had better check on his territory in the northwest part of the state.

Charlie had always enjoyed taking this road trip, as he could combine work with a visit to his younger brother, John, who lived on a ranch near Faith. Many individuals would not want to venture into his barren part of South Dakota, as Highway 212 was not paved and proved to be muddy during the spring rains, and very dusty in the summer months. In fact, most tourists would make their destination the Black Hills of South Dakota, and not venture this far north in the state.

Also, it was in this area that Charlie and his young wife first homesteaded with their parents after arriving from Corning, Iowa. Charlie's memories were of living in a sod house with nothing but a dirt floor and boards for a ceiling. In addition to not being able to make a living, his young wife, Beulah, did not like the barren flat ground surrounding their home. This had been the reason that Charlie applied for and accepted his first law enforcement job in Elk Point, South Dakota.

Chapter 14

Charlie's Visit to His Brother

After spending several days checking the numerous grocery stores and taverns along Highway 212 without incident, Charlie headed for his brother's ranch.

Now, John owned and operated a cattle ranch in northwest South Dakota near Faith. He was the youngest of the five Campbell boys, and existed on a cattle ranch that barely made enough money to meet expenses. In fact, in the late 1940s and early1950s, John and his wife, Floy, had a two-hole outhouse about twenty yards from the backdoor of their tar-paper, modest home.

John and Floy had no children to help with the many chores required to maintain this small homestead. Floy raised a few chickens and had a vegetable garden. During the summer months, the cattle would graze on the sparse grasslands of this barren part of the state. In the early fall, John would sell most of the herd to ranchers in the eastern part of the state who were able to raise corn to "fatten up" the stock before selling the herd to the stockyards in either Sioux City, Iowa, or Omaha, Nebraska.

John further supplemented their evening meals with bullhead fish that he stocked in his many dams. Now, bullheads are similar to catfish, but are smaller, and will tolerate the warm waters of the shallow dams dotting his many acres. The primary purpose of these dams was to supply water to the White-face Herefords.

Also, during the coldest part of the long winters, John would take an ice saw and cut blocks of ice to store in his dug-out storm cellar. The blocks of ice would be further insulated with straw to prevent their melting in the hot summers. As there was no electricity running to the home, John and Floy had a true icebox where the blocks of ice would keep perishable items cold.

Charlie had developed a love for fishing. Therefore, he and John would take bamboo poles with red floaters and fish for the bullheads. After skinning and cleaning the fish, Floy would roll the fish in cornmeal and fry the fish on the cast iron stove. With the fish, they would have fried potatoes that Floy had grown in her garden.

In the summer months, Floy would have fresh vegetables to place on the table. In the winter months, the vegetables would be from jars that Floy canned during the summer months.

Charlie would always bring a pint of their favorite whiskey, Jim Beam. Now, John and Charlie would have a slug or two before sitting down to dinner.

So that time would not be counted against his annual leave given to federal agents, Charlie would always drive his government car and pack a suit, a couple of dress shirts with ties, and city shoes. Of course, he carried his .38 revolver in his well-worn, tan suitcase.

After spending a night or two with John, Charlie would check some more grocery stores and bars in neighboring locations. Among the small bergs he would check would be Mud Butte, Faith, Maurine, Dupree, Red Elem, and Newell. All of these very small towns existed to supply the ranchers in the area with staples that they could not raise on their ranches.

There was only one time that Charlie had noticed a violation of the federal liquor regulations. That was in the grocery store in Mud Butte. It seemed that the owners had not purchased the necessary federal permit to sell liquor from their store. As Charlie was a personal friend of the couple who owned the store, he gave them two weeks to purchase and display the liquor permit. Charlie knew that it would probably be three weeks or more before he could schedule time to once again check businesses in this part of the state. Therefore, the Stevensons had plenty of time to comply with the regulation.

Chapter 15

Trouble in Eastern South Dakota

One evening as Charlie was preparing for his evening meal at home, he received a call from St. Paul. It was reported that the agent in charge of the territory east of the Missouri River suspected that a rather large illegal operation was in place.

As agents helped each other in time of need, Charlie was to pack his well-worn, tan suitcase and travel in his government car to Huron, South Dakota. First, he was to assist in discovering what was believed to be one of the largest illegal liquor operations in that part of the state. Then Charlie was ordered to help bring the law breakers to justice.

Beulah helped Charlie pack, as she always did when he departed on Monday mornings. Of course, he needed his shaving tote, a couple of clean shirts, a couple of ties, and three pairs of knee-high socks with garter supporters. On top of everything, he placed his .38

special revolver with shoulder holster. He carried his handcuffs in his suit coat pocket, along with a leather-wrapped lead club.

After arriving in Huron, he drove directly to Agent Johnson's office for a briefing. It seemed that just about every bar in Huron and the neighboring towns had a supply of un-taxed liquor that was being sold under-the-counter to recognizable customers. Agent Johnson had obtained this information from an unnamed source in the country. As the agents wanted to keep the identity of this individual secret, it was not revealed to anyone working the case.

Now the real difficult part was to find where the "moonshine" was being made. In past cases, the agents would "stake out" a particular bar and wait for the truck delivery. However, after several nights sitting in darkened cars at a couple of bars, the agents did not see any deliveries being made. It seemed that the agents would need to find the source of where the "moonshine" was being produced before they could determine just how the deliveries were being made at the individual bars undetected by the agents.

Many illegal brewers think that they can "outsmart" the law enforcement agencies. However, they some-times do not realize that the average law-abiding citizen knows what is going on in his or her community and will assist the law. This was the case when a farmer north of Huron suspected his new neighbor of unusual behavior. It seemed the new neighbor, by the name of Nabors, was not planting his crops on time in the spring and let his field go to weeds. This was most unusual in this community! Mr. Nabors had large trucks arriving several times a week, and many cars coming and going constantly.

Charlie and two other agents drove out to the farm in question. Something was definitely unusual there. They didn't want to be recognized as snooping, so they carefully hid the car in a wooded area not far from the house. Sure enough, there was a lot of activity going on at the house and barnyard. There was enough mystery to warrant a further investigation.

To follow up on Charlie's report, the agency obtained the necessary search warrants, and the assembled agents staged a raid. The raid was to take place about three in the morning, when they hoped everyone would be asleep.

Several government, state, and local police cars drove very slowly with their headlights turned off down the dirt road leading north out of Huron. The home was dark, and many officers in the raiding party thought that this would be an easy arrest. Little did they know that the criminals had posted a guard and had alerted all in the rural home of the approaching agents.

The criminals knew that their illegal operation was compromised and that they would be arrested. Therefore, they planted elaborate traps for the agents that would explode as soon as they entered the front or back door of the home or barn.

In the meantime, the criminals scampered across the field in the back of the house and made it to the small stream a few hundred feet away from the barn. They had several boats waiting and paddled downstream, before rowing to the river bank and getting into their waiting cars, making their escape.

It was unfortunate that an eager local policeman from Huron, by the name of McDonald, after announcing his arrival and ordering the door to be opened, twisted the front door handle of the home. As soon as the door was ajar, a mighty explosion rocked the entire area. The policeman was immediately killed, and those agents following closely behind were seriously injured.

It seemed that the criminals had triggered a trip-wire to a few sticks of dynamite. In addition to the explosion, the entire home was set ablaze. The alcohol in the home alone added to the mighty fire that destroyed the home in a matter of minutes.

Of course, all of the evidence was destroyed in the fire. The criminals were able to make it out of the state, and to this day, the case is still not solved. The "moonshine" was confiscated in the bars, and the owners of the bars were arrested. However, none of the bar owners would tell where they had been obtaining the liquor. Perhaps they were too terrified to testify. Even with the possibility of reduced sentences, none of the bar owners would break their oath of silence.

The funeral for the slain police officer from Huron was a solemn affair, with officers from across the state and nation coming to Huron to pay their last respects. As is the custom for fallen police officers, there was a bagpipe playing both before and after the service. In addition, the bagpipe played at the graveside. Of course, with the last name of McDonald, the bagpipe music was very appropriate.

After the traditional rifle salute, the casket was closed and the agents slowly made their way out of Huron and returned to their home offices. This event was especially difficult for the agents as they not only lost one of their own, but the perpetrators were never caught.

Chapter 16

The Terrorist in Kansas

Though the late 1940s and early 1950s were primarily a peaceful time in America, there always seemed to be some deranged individual who had a score to settle with either an individual, or perhaps the United States Government.

Such was the case of a recently released prisoner from the federal military prison at Fort Leavenworth, Kansas. Fred Osborn was dishonorably discharged from the Army after having been found guilty of engaging in establishing a prostitution and gambling operation in Paris, France.

Fred was a career soldier and had obtained the rank of Sergeant First Class. He was considered a hero in World War II after acts of valor in the Battle of the Bulge. However, the idea of making some really big money on prostitution and gambling in Paris was just too tempting to pass by.

Being stationed in Germany and having several leaves to visit Paris, France, he soon became friends with a few "seedy" French characters from the underworld. The newfound friends told Fred that they could obtain the "girls" and find a location for gaming operations if Fred could direct soldiers from his unit to visit Paris.

Soon, by word of mouth, Fred passed on information of where soldiers from his unit could obtain the best looking girls in Paris, and the price was very reasonable. He also told them that his "girls" were tested for any sexually transferable diseases by a local doctor whom he had hired. To "sweeten the pot," Fred would pay the train fare from their base in Germany to Paris. *"Boy, what a deal,"* thought many bored boys away from home.

As Fred's cut from this illegal operation was generous, he thought, *"Why not make a little more money by selling counterfeit Chanel Number Five perfume and silk scarves."*

Everything was going very smoothly for Fred until a poor farm boy from South Dakota lost his entire month's salary gambling, and in addition, had contracted a bad case of gonorrhea. After reporting to the base hospital, Private Applegate was persuaded by the base chaplain to tell the whole story of his trips to Paris and to leave nothing out, or else he could face several months in the base stockade.

A "sting operation" was set up in one of the brothels in Paris, and a number of soldiers were arrested. For leniency in their sentencing, they "spilled the beans" on Sgt. Osborn.

Appearing before a military court, Sgt. Osborn was stripped of his rank, received a "dishonorable discharge," and received a sentence of six years at Fort Leavenworth. In disgrace, Sgt. Osborn was shipped home in handcuffs, accompanied by two burly M.P.'s by the names of Corporal Gus and Sgt. Arnold.

It had occurred to Sgt. Osborn that he might escape by pretending to be sick and by using the restroom on the train. He could overpower one of the guards who always accompanied him when he went to the dining car or the restroom. This turned out to be a bad idea as when Sgt. Osborn tackled Corporal Gus around the waist, all the Corporal had to do was lay the butt of his pistol on the Sergeant's head, and that was the end of the fight. As the force of the hit on the head had opened a large gash on the prisoner's head, the accompanying guards had to find the train's porter to obtain gauze and bandages to place on Sgt. Osborn's head.

Now, Fred Osborn had been corresponding with his fiancée, Mary Eleanor, for several months. Mary's father had a very lucrative new car business in Seattle, Washington, and Fred had aspirations of joining the firm as soon as he finished this last tour of duty.

Because of his dishonorable discharge, former Sgt. Osborn lost all of his future retirement benefits. Then a "Dear John" letter from Mary Eleanor arrived as he was settling into his new home in a very small cell at Fort Leavenworth.

Sgt. Osborn thought that Army chow was terrible, but the slop that they served on tin plates at Fort Leavenworth was even worse. In fact, he would often find cockroaches under his mashed potatoes.

Sgt. Osborn had now lost everything he had hoped to achieve. Many men react to such events by withdrawing into a shell. However, it was the opposite for this big, burly man who was number 0128760, or "former" Sgt. Osborn. He tore up his cell, and while attacking a guard, inflicted such injuries that the guard spent two months in the hospital with a broken jaw and other multiple injuries. Of course, this resulted in Fred spending the next six weeks in isolation. During this time in the "hole," Fred thought of how he could "get even" with all of the individuals who had ruined his life.

In Fred's mind, he composed a list of who would receive their justified consequences. In the six weeks in the "hole," the list continued to grow and now consisted of at least five individuals.

Due to Fred's unruly behavior, he served the entire sentence and was approaching fifty years old when finally released from prison in December of 1953. With a few dollars from his widowed mother, he hitched a ride to Wenatchee, Washington. This little town was on the edge of the Cascade Mountains.

Fred had just enough money to obtain supplies and bought a .22 caliber pistol. Hiking the Cascades, he found an abandoned cabin in which to plot his revenge against Mary Eleanor's family.

As Mary Eleanor's family lived in Seattle, Fred had to find a way to travel to the family's home and seek his revenge for Mary Eleanor breaking off their approaching marriage. Fred thought that his former fiancée's family had plotted to talk Mary out of marrying this loser. Therefore, in Fred's twisted mind, he thought they all had to die. This would mean that Mary, her younger brother, and both parents were guilty in Fred's mind.

To obtain the money to buy a used car, some dynamite, and other essentials, Fred sold all of the items in the abandoned cabin. As this was a hunting cabin for a group of wealthy businessmen from Boise, Idaho, Fred could sell all of their hunting gear. He kept one rifle, a large knife, and a few other items he might need for his trip to Seattle.

Also, in the hunters' cabin he found a few sticks of dynamite. Fred thought to himself, "*Why would a group of hunters want dynamite?*" This mystery has never been solved.

On his solitary trip to Seattle, Fred was planning just how he would dispose of the family. With the dynamite, he thought he could blow up the estate of this wealthy family. As he had training in explosives, gained by his service in the Army, he knew how to "rig" the explosives so that they would explode without him being close to the home. Unfortunately for Mary Eleanor's family, Fred's plot succeeded, and the entire family lost their lives to a large explosion, followed by a fire that completely destroyed the residence.

Now the next target was his "snitch," Pvt. Applegate. Fred found out that Applegate lived in a little town in South Dakota by the name of Edgemont.

Traveling night and day while stopping only for gas and one meal a day, he arrived in Edgemont early one morning. Rather than call attention to having a stranger in town, he passed through Edgemont and found a cheap motel in Hot Springs, South Dakota.

Fred remembered that Applegate was an avid athlete and enjoyed jogging each morning about dawn. Now all he had to do was find out Applegate's route and "take him out" with a hunting rifle with a scope that one of the hunters had stored in their hunting cabin.

Driving through the little town of Edgemont, he finally found Applegate on the north side of town. This was going to be an easy hit, as Edgemont had only one policeman, and this early in the morning he was probably at home either sleeping or having breakfast.

Fred passed Applegate on the road, drove another mile, parked his car off a side road, and hid the car in a group of trees. He then waited in a ditch with his rifle to "take out" this snitch who had cost him his ideal life.

Taking careful aim, he slowly pulled the trigger and hit Applegate in the shoulder and stopped him cold. Not bothering to check to see that he was dead, Fred made a bee line for his car and rapidly drove out of town.

Now, everyone in this sleepy little town had heard the sharp discharge of the gun and came running out of their homes. One young lad was wise beyond his years and remembered the license number of the Washington state car. Running home, he wrote down the license and told his parents that the car was from the state of Washington, as he remembered the green lettering.

Somehow, Fred had driven through Hot Springs before authorities could stop him for the arrest. Now the chase was on to catch this would- be assassin. A call from the Fall River county sheriff to the state highway patrol and the Rapid City police alerted them that a shooter was on his way north.

It happened that Charlie was again enjoying his morning coffee and doughnuts when the call came through to the operator at the Rapid City police department. Why on this particular morning Charlie had strapped his .38 revolver into his side holster, he still could not remember. However, he joined the state police, county sheriff, and about six city police officers in setting up road blocks.

At this time, the authorities did not know if the assassin would be traveling on Highway 16 or 79 coming into Rapid City. Therefore, the law enforcement agents split their forces, and half took Highway 16 and the other half took Highway 79.

The officers manning the road blocks didn't wait long until they spotted the Washington car with Fred approaching. Instead of stopping, Fred broke through the roadblock by sideswiping the two parked patrol cars and kept on going. It was not until the chase arrived in downtown Rapid City that one of the officers managed

117

to shoot out one of Fred's tires. It was then that Fred bolted out of his car and ran down an alley behind Kansas City Street.

Charlie was still agile. He jumped out of one of the police cars and ran down the alley with his gun drawn. Together, they ran for about a block until Charlie knew that he would never catch the fleet-footed criminal. Therefore, with the intention of shooting over Fred's head, Charlie stumbled and hit Fred in the upper shoulder. Of course, with a .38 slug in his shoulder, this stopped Fred in his tracks. The wound was not life-threatening, and after being taken to St. John's Hospital, he had a guard placed in his hospital room.

* * * * *

After having a police officer involved in a shooting, the officer's gun is taken away from him, and he is placed on administrative leave until after an investigation. After what seemed to Charlie to be a rather long and unnecessary interview session with several witnesses, he was cleared by the local authorities. However, this was not enough for his district commander in St. Paul. The commander had to travel to Rapid City to further investigate the shooting. One question the commander asked was why Charlie was hanging out at the local police station instead of being on the road checking the federal liquor licenses.

Well, Charlie had to say goodbye to his frequent stops at the local police station for his coffee and rolls.

Anyway, he was somewhat behind on making his rounds and needed to be on the road again.

One happy conclusion to the story is that Applegate recovered from his wound and would continue his job as a civil service employee at Igloo, South Dakota. At Igloo, they stored shells and other explosives that had been used by the Army in both Korea and during World War II. Perhaps one interesting bit of information is that Tom Brokaw's father worked at Igloo as a bulldozer operator before moving his family to Yankton, South Dakota.

If you ask anyone living in this community, they will all have a different story to tell about the shooting that occurred one bright spring day in this little out-of-the-way berg.

Chapter 17

Conclusion

Charlie Campbell retired on June 30, 1954. However, this was not the end of the stories that his son, Calvin, heard. As Charlie had developed rheumatoid arthritis, he was not able to fulfill some of his wishes in retirement.

Charlie continued his love for fishing, and what better place to catch those beautiful rainbow trout than the Black Hills of South Dakota. Because of his declining health, Charlie could no longer drive a car, so Beulah would drive him to Canyon Lake, just on the outskirts of Rapid City, for fishing from the bank of the lake. Occasionally, a friend that he had worked with would be driving through Rapid City and stop and visit. Charlie had made many friends during his thirty years in law enforcement.

* * * * *

On one particular afternoon, a former ATF agent by the name of Ralph stopped to see Charlie at his home on Columbus Street. Now, Ralph had switched agencies from the ATF to the Secret Service.

Calvin was allowed to stay in the living room after supper and listen to Ralph's tales of his assignment in guarding Margaret Truman. It seemed that Ralph was not at all enamored with this assignment.

Regardless of what you may hear from other sources, Margaret was totally pampered by her father, President Harry Truman. In fact, when a newspaper reporter wrote a somewhat negative review of one of Margaret's piano concerts, the President called the reporter and raised "all kinds of hell." The President even called the editor and tried to have the reporter fired. Of course, the editor did not follow through with the firing of the reporter who gave the review.

In another incident, Ralph was expected to wait on Margaret as if the agent were her personal servant. The duties of a Secret Service agent are to provide protection – not to cater to the whims of a would-be debutant.

Perhaps these are unkind words, as this was in the past, but they were heard by a young boy many years ago.

* * * * *

In another incident years later, when Calvin was stationed at Fort Bliss Army Base in El Paso, Texas,

Beulah visited one weekend. Now, before leaving Rapid City, Charlie had asked her to "look up" an old friend who lived in El Paso. This agent had also switched agencies and was now a Border Patrol officer stationed in El Paso, with the responsibility for the border separating El Paso from Juarez, Mexico. As his children may still be living in El Paso, the author will not reveal the name of this agent, as what happened that night was rather foolish and dangerous.

After his wife had prepared dinner for the four of them, the agent asked Beulah and Calvin if they would like to visit Juarez. Of course, they could not say no to this invitation. Calvin had been over the border with his Army buddies; however, his mother had never been out of the United States.

There really is nothing to see in this poverty ridden Mexican town at night, except bars and strip joints. The bullfights are held in the afternoons.

Well, the three went from one bar to another, and with each drink, the agent became more belligerent and somewhat out of control. He evidently had a reputation as a tough agent, and it seemed all of the bar owners were somewhat afraid of him. Calvin even remembers that on the ride home, this agent had side-swiped a food cart and received a few cuss words from the vendor.

When Beulah and Calvin arrived at their motel in El Paso, Calvin apologized to his mother, and together they thanked their lucky stars that they had not spent the night in a Mexican jail.

* * * * *

Prior to Charlie Campbell developing a rather serious case of arthritis, he loved to take his black German Shepherd Pointer hunting dog and bag a few pheasants. Now, South Dakota is a prime location for pheasant hunting, and many hunters from other states will travel to South Dakota to hunt the local pheasants.

It was a very sad day when Charlie had to sell his hunting dog, as he was no longer able to hunt pheasants. However, Beulah would drive Charlie to his brother's cattle ranch, as John was still active and continued to hunt pheasants. With Charlie sitting in the car, he could watch John as he bagged a few pheasants that happened to be beside the road. With John's old Ford coupe, they even drove across the pasture lands to better scare up a few pheasants.

Charlie made the best of retirement, but it was not as he had imagined it to be, as he had looked forward to completing his thirty years of service with the ATF. Always an active man, it was very difficult for Charlie to adjust to a rather sedentary life style. Therefore, the moral of this story is to enjoy your life each day, as one's retirement years may not be as you might imagine.

* * * * *

My father, Charles E. Campbell, received the ALBERT GALLATIN AWARD for his outstanding service as both a Prohibition agent and later as an ATF agent. He served for over thirty years and retired on June 30, 1954. Albert Gallatin was the United States Secretary of the Treasury from 1801 until 1814. Mr. Gallatin stressed simplicity in government and termination of the public debt.

A copy of my father's highly prized certificate is now on display in Washington, D.C., along with the certificates of other members of the group of agents working under Mr. Eliot Ness.

Cal Campbell,
Author

Epilogue

Modern Expectations of an ATF Agent

Today, the job duties, qualifications, and expectations for the modern Alcohol, Tobacco, Firearms, and Explosives agent are far greater than what was required following the Prohibition days. Both the physical and educational qualifications are very strict for today's agents. Also, due to the terrorist threat, the duties have changed to reflect the current threat level in the United States.

It should be noted that to apply to be an agent, a person must wait until an announcement is made that the agency is accepting applications.

To begin with, an applicant must possess either a bachelor's degree in any subject area or have a combination of education and experience in law enforcement to qualify for the position.

There are presently 25 ATF field division offices throughout the United States. The prospective agent must apply at one of these locations.

The annual salary range for new agents is between $33,829 and $42,948. In addition, agents receive from 13 to 26 days of vacation per year. Also, agents earn 13 days of sick leave per year and may accumulate without limit. Of course, there are also 10 paid holidays.

An agent may retire at age 50 with 20 years of experience in the agency. However, the mandatory retirement age is 57.

To summarize, the requirements for becoming an agent are:

1. The applicant must be at least 21 years old and no older than 37 on the date of application.
2. The prospective agent must pass a pre-employment physical test (PIT). This test is very rigorous and demands that the man or woman must be in very good physical condition.
3. The applicant's weight must be in proportion to his or her height.
4. The applicant's vision must be at least 20/100 and corrected to 20/20.
5. A writing sample is required, in addition to a multitude of both written and oral examinations.
6. A hearing test will be administered.
7. Both a drug test and a polygraph exam are required.

8. The agency will not accept anyone with a felony record.
9. It should be noted that it is not uncommon for agents with many years of experience in the ATF to have a base salary of between $71,674 and $93,175.

The agents who are able to speak and understand a foreign language are paid more, and there is locality pay that is in addition to the base salary. The current range for locality pay is 14.16% to 35.25% of the base pay. (Evidently, a few agents are assigned to locations that are considered not the most desirable.)

To obtain more information, one should visit the agency's web site at www.atf.gov.

As a summary, my father would never have passed the new requirements. However, Charlie Campbell retired on June 30, 1954, and had a very distinguished career, as his award of the Albert Gallatin Certificate will verify.

Photographs

Picture Of A German Shepherd Dog That Looks Similar to Gary – Charlie's Dog In Elk Point

As this was Charlie Campbell's first position in law enforcement, it was indeed helpful to have the assistance of a very large German Shepherd to control Elk Point. This little town in southeast South Dakota, close to the Missouri River, had a few "bad apples" who needed to be controlled. Together, this tandem of constable and dog was all that was needed to keep a "tight lid" on those who might display unnecessary behavior.

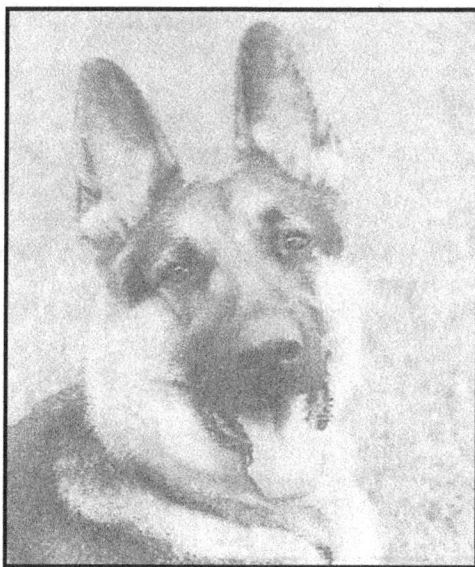

Charlie Campbell Becomes A Prohibition Agent

It was indeed fortunate that Charlie Campbell had an opportunity to join the elite force of Federal Agents who were given the assignment of enforcing Prohibition.

(Photo Supplied By Author)

132

Federal Agents With Sheriff
(Could be West Virginia)

Charlie Campbell is second row, second from right.

(Photo Supplied By Author)

Type of Car Used by the Bootleggers in West Virginia

The illegal moonshine had to be transported from the still to where the consumers were waiting to purchase the "White Lightning." It was necessary for the bootleggers to be able to outrun the Federal chase cars. Therefore, a fast car with plenty of space for carrying the "booze" became a necessity. The picture below shows the type of car used by the bootleggers.

(Photo Supplied By Author)

Type of Car Used by Agent Campbell in West Virginia

Agent Campbell arrived in West Virginia in a coupe similar to the one pictured below. Of course, the car was not in as good a condition and was covered in mud.

(Photo Supplied By Author)

Large Wooden Containers to Keep Moonshine

The bootleggers had an elaborate formula for making their illegal "booze." With practice, the criminal element was able to produce some liquor of questionable quality.

My father told me the vats holding the liquor were not always the cleanest and often, after draining the "booze," the Agents would find dead rats in the bottom of the wooden containers.

(Photo Supplied By Author)

Rum Runners: Key West

Serving as an Agent in Key West, Florida, was a totally new experience for Charlie Campbell. In fact, Charlie had not seen a body of water larger than Lake Michigan when stationed in Chicago. Below is a picture taken in the beautiful Keys.

(Photo Supplied By Author)

Ernest Hemingway Home in Key West

Charlie was invited to Ernest Hemingway's home for a fine meal of fresh grouper that had been caught that afternoon. Although Ernest had cleaned the fish, it was Ernest's wife Pauline who cooked the meal.

Perhaps the best part of the evening was the Jamaican rum that was served after the meal. I might add that the two men also enjoyed their Cuban cigars.

(Photo Supplied By Author)

Ernest Hemingway Kitchen Window

After catching fish, Ernest would clean the fish in his kitchen and throw the innards out of the kitchen window to the cats waiting outside.

(Photo Supplied By Author)

139

Sloppy Joe's Bar in Key West

Sloppy Joe's Bar is where Pauline Hemingway found the urinal that she had a workman bring back to her home and converted into a goldfish pond. As the bar owner was replacing the urinals, the workmen had the old ones stacked outside the bar on the sidewalk. Laying the urinal down in Hemingway's back yard, the workman placed decorative tiles on the outside. If you visit the Hemingway home today in Key West you will be able to view this most unusual goldfish pond.

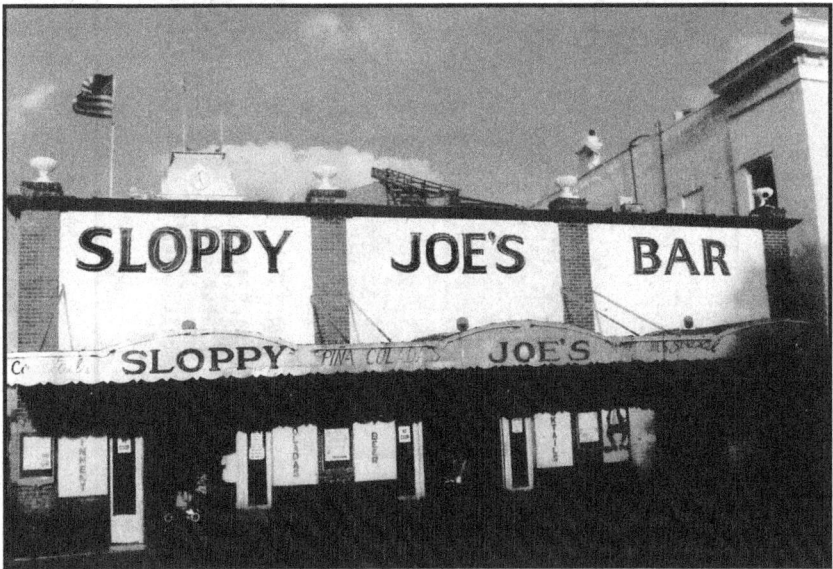

(Photo Supplied By Author)

Goldfish Pond in Back Yard of Hemingway Home

The goldfish pond was actually once a urinal in the men's room of Sloppy Joe's Bar in Key West. Notice the workman placed decorative tiles around the edge of the pond. The pond is located just outside the back door of the Hemingway home in Key West.

(Photo Supplied By Author)

Mahogany Boat Similar to One Used by Agents in Key West

Although not exactly the same type of boat as used by Charlie and Martino just off the shores of Key West, the boat is similar to the 1920's mahogany boat. Notice how small the very fast boat appears.

(Photo Supplied By Author)

The Civilian Conservation Corp

Prior to World War II young men had difficulty obtaining paying jobs. This included my older brother Edward Eugene. Therefore, when Charlie Campbell was stationed in Rapid City, Ed joined the corps and worked in a camp near Hill City, South Dakota. The young men were furnished small cabins, with as many as four young men sharing a very small cabin. Pictured below is an example of one of the CCC cabins.

(Photo Supplied By Author)

The Canadian Connection

The operation in Canada was unlike many of Charlie's operations as there would be no "moonshine" to confiscate. Rather, Scotland was exporting its good Scotch whiskey to Canada and then the criminal element was trucking the very fine whiskey into the United States without paying the U.S. Federal tax. The Scotch would arrive in large barrels and then be bottled in Canada. Below is a picture of one of the barrels.

(Photo Supplied By Author)

Piper J-3 Cub Used by
Federal Agents in Nebraska

The Piper J-3 Cub is a small, simple, light aircraft that was built between 1937 and 1947 by Piper Aircraft. This type of aircraft was used by Federal Agents in Nebraska as they searched for the dust trails of trucks carrying illegal "moonshine" in the Sand Hills of Nebraska. With tandem (fore and aft) seating the two Federal Agents soon were able to spot the trucks.

(Photo Supplied By Author)

Illegal Hooch: Close to Home

It was unusual for illegal liquor to be produced in Rapid City after Prohibition was repealed. However, when you combine prostitution with illegal "brew" and "White Lightning" the profits become substantial. Pictured below is a Victorian home similar to the one operating on West Boulevard. Both illegal activities were shut down by Agent Campbell and other law enforcement officers.

(Photo Supplied By Author)

Confiscated Liquor

It was unusual, but long after Prohibition was repealed a few individuals still made their own brew and "White Lightning." Of course, when the entrepreneurs combined the sale of the liquor with prostitution the profits doubled or sometimes tripled. Below is the confiscated barrels of liquor taken in Rapid City.

(Photo Supplied By Author)

Federal Agents with Local Police
(Could be Rapid City, South Dakota)

Charlie Campbell is second row, second from right.

(Photo Supplied By Author)

Agent Charlie Campbell Fishing with His Brother

It was always an event that Charlie looked forward to. Agent Charlie was long due for a few days of rest and he liked nothing more than to visit his brother John on his ranch in northwest South Dakota, near Faith. The little boy covering his eyes against the bright sun is Charlie's youngest son Calvin.

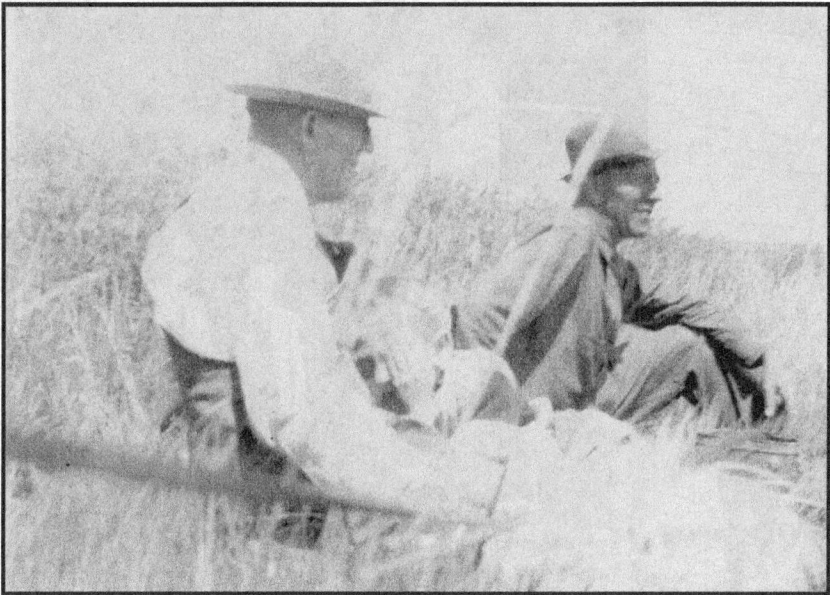

(Photo Supplied By Author)

Trouble in Eastern South Dakota

Although the evidence in Huron was destroyed in the fire, the agents thought that the elaborate set-up might have appeared as depicted in the following photos taken from another arrest earlier in the year in North Dakota.

Charlie Campbell is second Agent from right.

(Photo Supplied By Author)

Processing Machinery for Making Illegal Liquor

Many think the elaborate processing machinery for making illegal liquor resembled the machinery shown in this picture. Unfortunately, the evidence was destroyed in the fire in Huron.

(Photo Supplied By Author)

(Photo Supplied By Author)

(Photo Supplied By Author)

Newspaper Article

Local Man Helped Crack Some
Of Region's Big Prohibition Cases

C. E. Campbell is shown proudly displaying the Albert Gallatin Award presented him for 30 years service with the Treasury Department.

LETTERS OF COMMENDATION
PROMOTION
AND
AWARDS

CHARLES E. CAMPBELL

FEDERAL AGENT
ALCOHOL, TOBACCO AND
FIREARMS
TREASURY DEPARTMENT

TREASURY DEPARTMENT

INTERNAL REVENUE SERVICE

~~Sioux City, Iowa~~
Omaha, Nebraska,
August 13, 1927.

Mr. Charles E. Campbell,
Federal Prohibition Agent,
Omaha, Nebraska.

About 10 days ago I told you that I wanted to make a record on the capture of stills during the first 15 days of August, and you have certainly made that record. You began the work of making this record on Thursday, August 4th, and the drive comes to an end today, August 13th. In that time you have seized a total of 20 stills and run the total number of stills seized by this office since I took charge, December 15th, up to 104 stills.

I believe that the work which you seven men have done in the first half of August has never been equalled in the history of the Nebraska Prohibition Office. I want you to know how much I appreciate the strenuous efforts you have all made to make a success of this drive. I have reported the facts to the Administrator and feel very certain that he will be proud of the work done by you as Prohibition Agents.

Yours truly,

Elmer E. Thomas,
Acting Deputy Administrator.

EET:AVS

TREASURY DEPARTMENT

BUREAU OF INDUSTRIAL ALCOHOL

WASHINGTON

OFFICE OF
COMMISSIONER OF INDUSTRIAL ALCOHOL

ADDRESS REPLY TO
COMMISSIONER OF INDUSTRIAL ALCOHOL
AND REFER TO

FEB 2 1934

Mr. Charles E. Campbell,
   117 S. Pine Street,
      Vermillion, South Dakota.

Dear Sir:

    It is probable that this Bureau will organize, in the near future, a field force of Inspectors to be assigned to regulative duties (not to the inspection of permittees). Their duties will be very similar to those performed by Prohibition Agents under the former Bureau of Prohibition, the important difference being that their activities will be confined to those states which have legalized the manufacture and sale of liquor, and the purpose will be to see that no liquor is made or sold without the proper Federal taxes being paid thereon.

    Appointments to these positions will be at an entrance salary of $2600, with per diem in lieu of subsistence at the rate of $5 per day when in a travel status. If you are interested in appointment to such a position, please fill out the enclosed application blank and return it at once to this office.

    By direction of the Commissioner of Internal Revenue:

                    Very truly yours,

                    D. S. Bliss,
           Commissioner of Industrial Alcohol.

Encl.
ecc

TREASURY DEPARTMENT

BUREAU OF INDUSTRIAL ALCOHOL

WASHINGTON

OFFICE OF
COMMISSIONER OF INDUSTRIAL ALCOHOL

ADDRESS REPLY TO
COMMISSIONER OF INDUSTRIAL ALCOHOL
AND REFER TO

April 10, 1934

AAP:MC

Mr. Charles E. Campbell,
   c/o District Supervisor,
     St. Paul, Minnesota.

Sir:

    The Civil Service Commission having authorized your permanent reinstatement, you are hereby appointed, with the approval of the Secretary of the Treasury, effective date of oath, an Inspector, Bureau of Industrial Alcohol, in the field service generally throughout the United States or its territorial possessions, for temporary assignment to duty under the direction of the District Supervisor, District No. 8, St. Paul, Minnesota.

    You will receive compensation at the rate of $2600 per annum (CAF-7) and be allowed $5.00 per diem in lieu of actual expenses for subsistence, together with actual and necessary traveling expenses, subject to the limitations prescribed by law and regulations, when absent on official business from your designated post of duty, payable from the appropriation, "Salaries and Expenses, Bureau of Industrial Alcohol."

    This letter of appointment is not to be accepted as credentials and any person approached by you in your official capacity is entitled, on demand, to view the regular departmental credentials in the form of a pocket commission.

    By direction of the Commissioner of Internal Revenue:

                 Respectfully,

                 D. E. Bliss,
        Commissioner of Industrial Alcohol.

Justification No. 8743

159

OFFICE OF
SUPERVISOR OF PERMITS
DISTRICT No

IN REPLY REFER TO

TREASURY DEPARTMENT

BUREAU OF INDUSTRIAL ALCOHOL

St. Paul, Minnesota,
May 29, 1934.

To Inspectors (Regulative):

By direction of the Commissioner of Internal Revenue, and with the approval of the Secretary of the Treasury, your designation, heretofore known as "Inspector" (Regulative), in the Alcohol Tax Unit, Bureau of Internal Revenue, will, effective June 1, 1934, be changed to "Investigator", without change in duties, salary or grade.

S. B. Qvale
Acting District Supervisor
District 8.

SBQ:hkk

State of South Dakota

Office of Attorney General

Know All Men By These Presents, That

C. E. Campbell   Investigator A. T. U.
Rapid City, S. Dak.

has completed a General Course of Instruction afforded by the Attorney General of the State of South Dakota, in conjunction with the South Dakota Sheriffs' and Police Officers' Association and the Federal Bureau of Investigation, and that he is entitled to such professional standing as a law enforcement officer as may be properly accorded by reason of the completion by him of such course of instruction.

Dated this ___12___ day of ___May___ 19__38__

_____
Attorney General

_____
Secretary, South Dakota Sheriffs'
and Police Officers' Association

ATTEST: _____
Secretary of State

161

𝕌𝕟𝕚𝕥𝕖𝕕 𝕊𝕥𝕒𝕥𝕖𝕤 𝕋𝕣𝕖𝕒𝕤𝕦𝕣𝕪 𝔻𝕖𝕡𝕒𝕣𝕥𝕞𝕖𝕟𝕥

ALBERT GALLATIN AWARD
Charles Edward Campbell

Upon your retirement from the Federal service, this award is presented as an evidence of the esteem in which you are held by the Treasury Department, which has been the principal beneficiary of your labors for so many years.

The fine contribution you have made to the public service well merits this commendation of your Government.

Signed in the City of Washington, D.C.

June 30, 1954

Secretary

TEXT
UNITED STATES TREASURY DEPARTMENT

ALBERT GALLATIN AWARD
To Charles Edward Campbell

Upon your retirement from the Federal service, this award is presented as an evidence of the esteem in which you are held by the Treasury Department, which has been the principal beneficiary of your labors for so many years.

The fine contribution you have made to the public service well merits this commendation of your Government.

Signed in the City of Washington, D.C.
June 30, 1954

Secretary

About Albert Gallatin

GALLATIN, ALBERT (1761-1849), A distinguished American public financier. He was born in Geneva, Switzerland, moving to the United States in 1780. In 1783, he purchased land on the western frontier of Pennsylvania, and in the following year opened a country store in Fayette County, Pennsylvania. In 1789, he was a delegate to the state constitutional convention, and from 1790 - 93 he was a member of the Legislature. From 1795 to 1801 he was a member of the Pennsylvania assembly, where he gradually rose to be its acknowledged leader. In 1801 Gallatin became Secretary of the Treasury, which position he held until 1813, rendering most valuable service. From 1816 to 1823 he was Minister to France, and three years later he went to London as United States Minister, remaining one year. He was nominated for the vice-presidency in 1824, but withdrew in behalf of Clay. In 1843 he declined to enter Tyler's cabinet as Secretary of the Treasury, and removed to New York.

From - New Standard Encyclopedia

CPSIA information can be obtained
at www.ICGtesting.com
Printed in the USA
FSOW03n1935230915
11473FS

9 781608 624317